HOT KNIVES

Lust for LEAF

ALEX BROWN

EVAN GEORGE

VEGGIE CROWD-PLEASERS TO FUEL YOUR PICNICS, POTLUCKS, AND RAGERS

PHOTOGRAPHS BY AARON FARLEY

Da Capo
LIFE
LONG

A Member of the Perseus Books Group

Design: Jen Wick Design Studio

Typeset in HFJ Whitney and Vitesse

Cataloging-in-Publication data for this book is available from the Library of Congress.

First Da Capo Press edition 2013

ISBN 978-0-7382-1697-3 (paperback)

ISBN 978-0-7382-1698-0 (e-book)

Library of Congress Control Number: 2013930052

Published by Da Capo Press

A Member of the Perseus Books Group

www.dacapopress.com

Da Capo Press books are available at special discounts for bulk purchases in the U.S. by corporations, institutions, and other organizations. For more information, please contact the Special Markets Department at the Perseus Books Group, 2300 Chestnut Street, Suite 200, Philadelphia, PA, 19103, or call (800) 810-4145, ext. 5000, or e-mail special.markets@perseusbooks.com.

10 9 8 7 6 5 4 3 2 1

No party is any fun unless
seasoned with folly.

—*Erasmus Desiderius*

IT ALWAYS CREEPS UP ON FRIDAY afternoon. You watch the week tick its way to beer o'clock, waiting for the payoff. After the hump (day); humping. After the rain; the rainbow. It's an itch begging to be scratched. A desire for drunken revelry. A powerful lust for the company of comrades, deep glasses, and full plates.

Yes, we lust after our friends, and we wanna cook for them the morning after—no, not like *that*. Hardwired in us all is a deep craving for communal consumption, whether that means huddling around a campfire with sticks, nibbling tea sandwiches in Sunday's best, or letting loose and breaking champagne flutes at a sweaty base-ment party. We relish our weekends. No, but we literally *relish* them—we slather minced pickles all over our days of rest and we wipe our hands on our shorts.

We prefer to live every weekend like it's our frat's last toga party. But we replace the bongs with tongs, the hand jobs with zipping hot fresh corn, and the beer pong table with a beat-up Weber grill—that's our idea of a bro-down.

As food blogging, former line cooks who have staked our claim to catering blow-out backyard parties and treating all our friends to drunken brunch exper-iments, writing a party food cookbook was not a stretch. As long as we've been friends, we've thrown parties

> As long as we've been friends, we've thrown parties together and treated it like a real job. We've been researching *Lust for Leaf* since before we were legal.

together and treated it like a real job. We've been researching *Lust for Leaf* since before we were legal. On the Hot Knives blog, parties are often the scene of our most brilliant, studied work.

Few things are as liberating as ap-proaching a raging outdoor party. The walks up a long flight of stairs while you're clutching a cold sixpack and still hidden from sight. When you can just listen to laughter coming from a gaggle of friends upon whom you're about unleash a high-five assault. You enter. Cheers and applause! You drop the sixer and anything else standing between you and kisses and hugs. Someone jabs a charred asparagus spear at your face, then

> Parties don't throw themselves. They require planning, prepping, and, sometimes, praying (for a party). But don't worry, that's why we're here. We are your bearded, mezcal-swilling Marthas.

someone else tilts a tequila bottle to your lips. And there you are, joining blissful oblivion.

Garden parties, birthday parties, or seemingly self-starting get-togethers that spring up for no other reason than it's warm enough to swim in the pool. We need to lose ourselves in the heat of hanging out. It makes perfect sense that this urge comes on hotter in spring and summer. If winter holidays are about giving thanks, self-reflection, and new beginnings, summer sessions are the opposite: living whole hog, no thinking about anything other than whether the fire is hot enough to put cool fucking grill marks on a lamb-sized leek. (We do not condone winter barbecuing in a basement, but hey, do what you got to do.)

But here's the rub. This communal oblivion we prize is a fragile achievement. It's not guaranteed and it doesn't happen on its own. Parties don't throw themselves. They require planning, prepping, and, sometimes, praying (for a party). But don't worry, that's why we're here. We are your bearded, mezcal-swilling Marthas. Stewarts, we mean. All we ask is that you put our advice to good use. Pamphlet the neighborhood, call up your homies, and invite everyone you love, because before you know, it will be Monday.

Fire Walk With Us

The Thermodynamics of Cool

If you can start a fire, you can do anything: burn down your house, warm your toes, or feed an army of your smelly friends. The essential act of harnessing unbridled energy simultaneously time-warps you back to our nomadic protohuman roots and reifies the totality of civilization in swift, smoky strokes. Because we make fire, we are advanced. Because we can channel it to make things delicious, we are fucking gods.

That said, not everybody is good at starting a cooking fire. Frankly, most people suck at it. We're certain an image of three to six dudes huddled around a grill or a campfire pit scratching their beards and stabbing at a smoldering pile of lighter fuel–soaked briquettes just came to mind. This common calamity has likely led many away from their Cro-Mag roots toward the shiny and expensive ease of the gas powered "grill," which surreptitiously robs you, your food, and your guests of 90 percent of the glory and good of outdoor cooking. The ritual of the ages is lost with a twist of the wrist and a neutered electric click, and even though you can "grill" with gas, you can't ever take it with you into the semi-wild urban outdoors.

So ditch the technological ball and chain and step into the sun, where all you need is a bag of coals, a grill, and few tricks. Armed thusly, there'll be no party you can't best. Learning the essentials of taming the untamed element will quickly elevate you to Doctor status, casting you in the bronze of the ages as the one who can control that which cannot be controlled.

Fire Kit Essentials: Three Cs

COALS

Find real coals made from wood. Mesquite coals are readily available these days at a random cross section of liquor stores, hardware shops, and bodegas. Seek and ye shall find. It's worth it. Your fire, your food, and your lungs will be free of chemicals and all their ills. If you need to resort to Kingsford, look for the stuff without lighter fluid. You don't need it.

CHIMNEY STARTER,

a.k.a. the smartest thing ever made. Created in the 1960s by three dudes who were obsessed with a dream they initialized as the "Auto Fire," this gizmo lets even the most uninitiated outdoor cook show up every Eagle Scout on the block— and it generally costs less than $60. While chimney starters are not exactly compact, they are super light. Take 'em camping, to work, to the streets. But, like, always use them responsibly or whatever.

CITRUS

Getting those grill bars clean is as simple as slicing a lime or lemon and grabbing a set of tongs. After your grill is searing hot, carefully press and rub a halved lime or lemon back and forth and you'll clear away any detritus that you were too wasted to deal with last summer. Toss the greased half-fruit into the flames as a burnt offering to the gods of clean.

Food Pyramid

Enjoy your food, but party harder. Eat everything with your hands. Drink booze and fruit, not water. Make all of your junk food yourself. Cook at least half of everything you eat on an open fire. Switch to uppers, if possible.

These are just a few of the obscure, codified dietary restrictions that define how we eat on weekends, but really there's just one rule you should follow: Don't eat alone. Done correctly, your Sabbaths should be a heat-stroke blur of communal feasts strung together by barbecue tans.

With your health in mind, Hot Knives has performed dietary research more extensive than the Food and Drug Administration (or the Bureau of Alcohol Tobacco and Firearms for that matter). Our findings suggest a steady diet of these seven food groups may lead to a stronger immune system, increased mental prowess, improved sex life, and the general amping up of your lust for life. In each food group, be sure to consume daily servings of the following:

Bro-tein

- DIY wieners and patties
- Brain-dead Americana
- Saucey explosions
- PG. 51

Potlatches

- Spicey ricey, steamy beany
- Unwilting salads
- Picnic blanket brunch comas
- PG. 79

(V) = VEGAN

Converting to Metric

TEMPERATURE
To convert from Fahrenheit to Celsius, subtract 32 and multiple by .56.
212°F = 100°C
225°F = 110°C
250°F = 120°C
275°F = 135°C
300°F = 150°C
350°F = 180°C
375°F = 190°C
400°F = 200°C
425°F = 220°C

LIQUID VOL UME
1 teaspoon = 5 milliliters (ml)
1 tablespoon = 15 ml
1 cup = 240 ml
1 quart = .95 liters (l)
1 gallon = 3.8 l

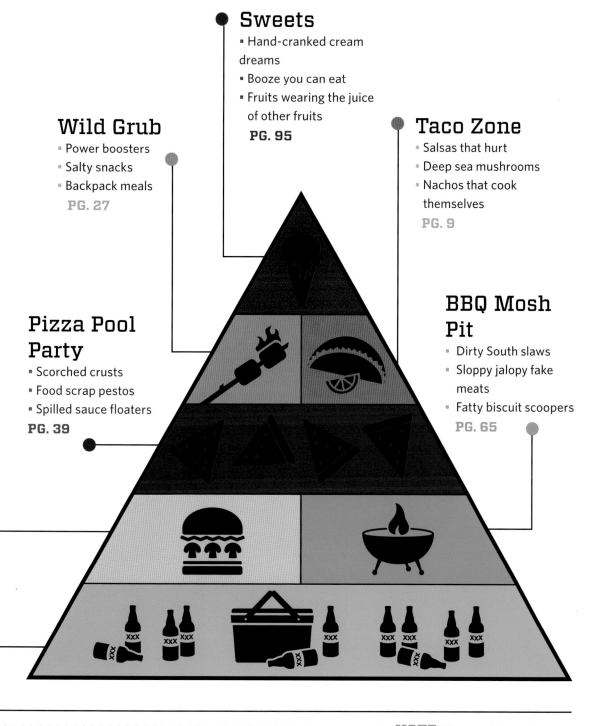

Sweets
- Hand-cranked cream dreams
- Booze you can eat
- Fruits wearing the juice of other fruits

PG. 95

Wild Grub
- Power boosters
- Salty snacks
- Backpack meals

PG. 27

Taco Zone
- Salsas that hurt
- Deep sea mushrooms
- Nachos that cook themselves

PG. 9

Pizza Pool Party
- Scorched crusts
- Food scrap pestos
- Spilled sauce floaters

PG. 39

BBQ Mosh Pit
- Dirty South slaws
- Sloppy jalopy fake meats
- Fatty biscuit scoopers

PG. 65

WEIGHT
1 ounce = 28 grams
1 pound (lb) = .45 kilograms (kg)
2.2 lbs = 1 kg

LENGTH
¼ inch (in) = .6 centimeters (cm)
½ in = 1.25 cm
1 in = 2.5 cm

NOTE: Hey you, Brits and Euro-users, don't know what the fuck 2 cups looks like? This is your key to make partying with California produce a Bi-Continental experience!

Taco Zone

WE USED TO WORSHIP THREE NIGHTS A WEEK AT THE TRASH-STREWN ALTER OF LEO'S TACOS, OUR LATE-NIGHT TACO TRUCK. Leo obliged us bleary-eyed kids who ordered the "vegetarian taco, no cheese" with **two hot corn silver dollars topped with richly salted pintos** and flicks of cilantro and no-joke green chile. One night we watched him swat away a gang-bang brawl with his spatula. His food taught us that **feeling bad the next morning should never get in the way of feeling good the night before.**

Which is where the proper hot salsa bar comes in. Whether sauce is slapped on your plate or **laid out for you in paint buckets like pig troughs**, we expect a fiery red, tangy green, pickled chiles, cool knobby radishes, and a crema to soothe all pains.

Call us un-American (please) but we think tacos say Fourth of July because they're the **perfect bootstrap food**. So once we've iced down a bucket of American beer, and obtained all the fireworks we can carry, we light up our grill in a tricolor rainbow of red, white and green salsa fixings. And we follow another taco truck tenet: **we eat it all on the curb.**

Verdugo Verde Ⓥ

Makes about 4 cups

5 medium-sized tomatillos (with skins on)
2 yellow wax peppers
1 poblano pepper
1 jalapeño
½ white onion (with peel)
3 scallions
⅛ cup lime juice
1 tablespoon olive oil, plus extra for brushing
2 large leaves iceberg lettuce
half a fuerte avocado
1 cup cilantro leaves
sea salt to taste

1. Once your grill is hot, brush tomatillos, peppers, and scallions with a bit of olive oil and sprinkle them with half a teaspoon of salt. Place 'em on the grill. Toss the half onion on without removing the peel. You want some blackened color so let cook for several minutes before gingerly flipping (remove tomatillos before they burst open and lose their juicy guts).

2. After blackening on both sides, remove all the veggies and let them rest for several minutes so they can cool.

3. Rub off any blackened skin and roughly peel. Roughly chop the veggies. Add them to a blender with 1 cup cilantro, the avocado, and the lime juice. Pulse for 1 minute, drizzling in 1 tablespoon of olive oil. Add the iceberg lettuce while pulsing. Salt to taste. Serve room temperature.

Radish Remoulade Ⓥ

Makes about 3 cups

2 cups veganaise
1 bunch of radishes
⅛ cup minced chives
1 tablespoon lime juice
sea salt to taste
1 tablespoon black pepper (or more if desired)

1. Pop each radish off from its leafy stem and wash thoroughly in a bowl of water, then strain and pile on your cutting board. Mince the radishes one at a time as thinly as possible: slice lengthwise four times, then set two of the slices aside while stacking the remaining two, then slice this stack lengthwise again, and rotate to slice width-wise. Repeat until you have a pile of tiny radish cubes.

2. Combine the radishes with veganaise, minced chives, and lime juice and stir. Crack more fresh black pepper than seems necessary and salt to taste.

Demon Seeds ⓥ

Makes about 4 cups

- 2 pounds ripe red tomatoes
- 5 dried New Mexico red chiles
- 3 jalapeños
- 1 red onion, unpeeled
- 1 tablespoon olive oil
- 1 clove garlic, peeled
- 2 tablespoons lime juice
- 2 tablespoons sesame seeds
- 2 teaspoons sesame oil
- 1 teaspoon olive oil,
  plus extra for brushing
- sea salt to taste

1. Once your grill is hot, brush tomatoes and jalapeños with a bit of olive oil, sprinkle with half a teaspoon of salt, and place on the grill. Toss on the onion whole, including skin. Turn veggies after several minutes. You want some blackened color on the tomatoes (but remove them before they burst and ejaculate their juice). Once jalapeños are charred remove them too. Rest the veggies for several minutes to let cool. Remove onion once the peel is charred.

2. Rehydrate your dried red chiles by placing them in a long flat-bottomed container and covering with about 2 cups of hot water. Let sit for at least 5 minutes, pressing down to keep covered.

3. Roughly chop the grilled tomatoes and jalapeños. Add them to a blender with 1 clove garlic and the lime juice. Pry out the grilled onion by slicing one of the tips off and applying pressure on the other end. Chop it and add to the blender. Remove your rehydrated chiles from their bath, roughly chop and add to the mix. Pulse for a minute, drizzling with the sesame and olive oil. Taste with a spoon and salt to taste.

4. In a small sauté pan on medium heat, toast the sesame seeds until golden, being careful to not to burn them. Add to the salsa and give it one more quick pulse to incorrorate.

Beverage

Eagle Rock,
Solidarity

Soundtrack

"Fire in Cairo,"
The Cure

Jackfruit Carnitas Ⓥ

Serves 12 to 15

"Little meats," (carnitas, translated into English) sounds perverted but perhaps no more so than "little banana pistons." When we first tried to make a stewed "pork," we used fresh banana flowers, and it was a mixed bag: not bad, exactly, but it took so fucking long to pry the flowery rods out of their phallic casings. Brined jackfruit, on the other hand, is black magic in a can: rinse, dry, and cook out some of the soggy brine and replace it with delicious sauce. At the risk of making this magic trick complicated, we smoke the jackfruit over wood chips, then stew it in fiery red chile. It can be made the night before or the morning of your taco party, then simply reheated over a stove, campfire, or grill. It's always worth the three-hour routine just to watch our friends take a bite and make a face like their brains've imploded. Follow these instructions and your friends will worship you too, like they just solved the worlds' mysteries or saw the Virgin of Guadalupe in a piece of fruit.

Beverage

Mikkeller,
Tomahawk

Soundtrack

"Hollywood
Babylon,"
the Misfits

RED CHILE SAUCE

2 cups dried red chile powder
   (California chile)
4 cups vegetable stock
¼ cup orange juice
⅓ cup grapeseed oil
1 white onion, chopped
half a head of garlic,
   peeled and minced
1 tablespoon cumin
1 teaspoon dried sage
1 teaspoon turmeric
½ teaspoon cinnamon
½ teaspoon coffee
1 ½ tablespoons all-purpose flour
4 chipotle peppers, in adobo

"CARNITAS"

2 handfuls of hickory wood chips
5 cans jackfruit, in brine
¼ cup grapeseed oil
half a head of garlic, minced
1 white onion, chopped

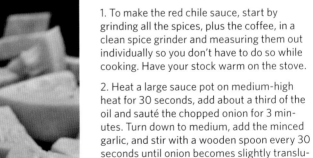

1. To make the red chile sauce, start by grinding all the spices, plus the coffee, in a clean spice grinder and measuring them out individually so you don't have to do so while cooking. Have your stock warm on the stove.

2. Heat a large sauce pot on medium-high heat for 30 seconds, add about a third of the oil and sauté the chopped onion for 3 minutes. Turn down to medium, add the minced garlic, and stir with a wooden spoon every 30 seconds until onion becomes slightly translucent, about 5 minutes.

3. Now drizzle another third of the oil to cover the whole cooking surface, followed by half the red chile powder, shake and stir to keep from burning and cook this for 3 minutes. (It should appear dark brown and disturbingly

clumpy, that's fine, just keep stirring lightly.) Toss in ground cumin, sage, turmeric, cinnamon ,and coffee while stirring. Chop your canned chipotle and add too. Finally add the rest of the oil and the flour, stirring and cooking another minute. With a ladle add about a cup of vegetable stock and use a whisk to mix while cooking for about 1 minute. Repeat two times. When you have 1 cup of stock left to add, assess whether the sauce is too thick or just about right and add accordingly. Add the orange juice and taste. It should be slightly bitter but balanced with the spices. Add salt to taste. Reserve until use.

4. While you prepare the jackfruit for smoking, soak the wood chips in water for about 20 minutes. Gently remove the jackfruit pieces (whole) from the can and drain over the sink in a colander. Rinse well with water to wash off excess brine and let sit in the sink for several minutes to drip dry. Set aside for grilling.

5. Prepare your outdoor grill (pg. 6). Drain wood chips and let them dry for 5 minutes. Pile the hot coals to one side of the grill then cover this red hot pile with the wood chips.

(You want a low to medium heat so you don't overcook the jackfruit.) Once ready, lay whole jackfruit pieces onto the grill and cover, leaving any vent holes ajar. Cook this way for an hour. Flip jackfruit and cook a second hour. You want a light blackening on some pieces. Remove and let cool.

6. Back in the kitchen...Break up the jackfruit pieces over a bowl by squishing hard between your thumb and forefingers. (They should be dry outside but slightly moist inside.) Place a large skillet on medium-high heat and divide the jackfruit into two batches: sweat half the onion for 3 minutes, add half the jackfruit, and cook like this for 10 minutes, stirring occasionally. Add half the minced garlic and cook for another 3 minutes before removing to a bowl. Repeat with the second batch.

7. Add the jackfruit and onion to a thick-bottomed pot and cover it with the red chile sauce. (You can let cool on the counter then fridge it overnight, or use it right away.) To reheat for serving, throw the pot on the stove or grill, stirring often, until it's piping hot.

////////////

HEY YOU!

No time to smoke your fruit? Dry it out on trays under low heat in the oven. Bottom line: evaporate that brine.

////////////

Aguas Frescas

OK, OK, OK ITS TRUE: WE DO DRINK THINGS OTHER THAN BEER.
But offer us fruit water, not tap water. When the weather turns from temperate to
sweltering, aguas frescas are also a great way to push the limits of your fruit in-
take, and get rid of anything that you bought too much of at the market. A word of
warning though: don't use fruit that you've held onto for too long. Just like pickling,
juicing is not for produce that's over the hill. All three of these recipes make for
bright, concentrated juices that you can stretch out with extra water and sweet-
ener. The base flavors can handle some dilution, so if you're having a party, just
stage them with lots of ice so they stay super cold, knowing that as the ice melts
the flavors will mellow. And yes, they all do well when spiked.

Each makes about a gallon

Horchata

4 cups white rice
5 cups raw almonds
1 gallon filtered water
2 cinnamon sticks
2 cups sugar
1 teaspoon nutmeg
2 teaspoons vanilla extract (pg. 106)

1. Toast the cinnamon sticks in a skillet over medium heat for 3 to 5 minutes, or until fragrant.

2. Soak the stuff overnight. Cover the rice and the almonds in 4 quarts of water in a container with a lid. Add toasted cinnamon sticks.

/////////// **24 Hours Later** ///////////

3. In your blender, pulverize the rice and almonds one cup at a time, with about 3 cups of the soaking water. If you run out of the water that they soaked in, just use extra filtered water. Strain this pureed "milk" into your serving vessel using a fine mesh strainer. Press the leftover solids with a spatula to get as much liquid out as you can. Return the leftover solids to whatever you used to soak them and cover with double their volume in water. Reblend and restrain, then discard the solids.

4. Season the milk with your nutmeg and the vanilla extract, then blend in the sugar. Taste for seasoning; you may want it sweeter or less so. Dilute liberally with water or ice accordingly, or grab some more sugar.

Suggested Saucing: rum, bourbon, and (in a pinch) reposado tequila.

Cantaloupe

2 ripe cantaloupes
20 leaves lemon verbena
3 quarts water
½ cup honey

1. In a small saucepan, combine 1 quart of water with the lemon verbena and heat just until boiling. Turn off the heat and whisk in the honey. Cool it.

2. Skin and seed your melons, and then process in a juicer, or by chopping the fruit into cubes and blasting in a blender. Use water from your remaining 2 quarts to blend.

3. Combine the cantaloupe juice and the verbena tea; taste for sweetness and ice it down.

Suggested Saucing: milder Scotches, vodka, tequila, mezcal.

Watermelon-Strawberry Ⓥ

1 ripe watermelon (preferably seedless)
6 baskets of strawberries
1 cup cilantro leaves
1 gallon water
1 cup sugar

1. Skin the watermelon; if it has a ton of seeds try to scrape them out. Process the watermelon in a juicer or in a blender with enough water to make it move.

2. Snip the stems off the strawberries and puree them to hell. Combine both fruit juices in a large vessel. Blend in the remaining water and the sugar.

3. Mince the cilantro and add it. Check for sweetness, ice the whole lot down, and serve.

Suggested Saucing: Gin.

Corn Porn

Serves 12 to 15

People don't believe us when we declare our unbridled love for Frito Pie—the South West's version of meatloaf—but we're serious. Alex grew up on the stuff and Evan's an easy convert to anything involving the Frito, which with its three ingredients (corn, salt, corn oil) is vegan and relatively crap-free. At the risk of scrubbing all the blue from its collar, we like to sex up this classic in something we call Corn Porn, or a corn "foursome": corn chips are on the bottom, a corn chile rides in the middle, then there's a fresh salad of herbed corn kernels getting nasty with a creamy dollop of corn fungus crema. What's corn fungus? It's a disease that grows on corn, which is way less fun to say than its other name, "huitlacoche," but it's delicious. Sub veganaise for safer sex. Or drop the topping if you can't find huitlacoche at your local Mexican carniceria or specialty store; there's nothing wrong with a corn three-way.

CHILE CON CORN
4 orange tomatoes
4 cups vegetable stock
4 ears of corn
half a habanero chile, minced
4 stalks of celery
1 yellow onion
1 yellow bell pepper
1 15-ounce can cannellini beans
3 tablespoons tomato paste
1 tablespoon olive oil
1 teaspoon turmeric, ground
1 teaspoon coriander, ground
2 bay leaves
sea salt to taste
3 1-pound bags of Fritos

SWEET CORN SALAD
2 ears of corn
2 scallions
1 bunch cilantro
1 lime
1 tablespoon olive oil
black pepper to taste

CORN SMUT CREAM
10 ounces huitlacoche
1 teaspoon cumin seeds
half a white onion
12 ounces labneh
½ teaspoon mace, nutmeg works
sea salt to taste

Beverage
Firestone Walker,
Velvet Merlin

Soundtrack
"Love on a Plate,"
Glass Candy

1. Start with a soup base for the chili: lightly char the tomatoes on the grill or under your stove's broiler. Once cool, combine the tomatoes with the vegetable stock in a blender and pulse until pureed.

2. Chop your onion and slice the corn kernels off with one downward knife motion over a large cutting board or mixing bowl. Place a thick-bottomed soup pot on medium heat, and add olive oil, followed by onion. Sweat the onion for 3 minutes, then add the corn and habanero. Stir every 30 seconds, while chopping the celery and mincing the garlic, then add both. Continue to stir. Chop and add the yellow pepper, turmeric, and coriander. Cook for another 3 minutes and stir. Add the tomato-broth base into the pot and cover.

3. Let cook for 5 to 8 minutes until it reaches a boil, then reduce to a simmer and add the cannellini beans, tomato paste, and two bay leaves. Salt it lightly, keeping in mind that Fritos are salty. Keep warm until serving.

4. For the sweet corn salad: cut off kernels from two more ears of corn (like above) and combine with chopped cilantro and scallions

thinly sliced on a bias. Toss with freshly squeezed lime juice, olive oil, and black pepper.

5. For the corn smut cream: toast the cumin seeds in a sauté pan for 2 minutes, tossing often. Chop the onion and toss it into the pan after you add olive oil. Cook this for several minutes. Add the huitlacoche and cook for another 3 minutes, tossing and smelling, then set aside to let cool. Once it's no longer hot,

combine the huitlacoche in a food processor with the labneh. Pulse for about a minute, scraping down the sides with a spatula if needed. Add nutmeg and sea salt to taste. Spoon this into a pastry bag or squirt bottle.

6. To serve: place Fritos at the bottom of a bowl, smother with chile, add a spoonful of sweet corn salad, and finally top with a generous squirt of the corn smut cream.

Hot Guac
to fry or not to fry

One raging debate among our close friends (they have to be close, you're about to know why...) is whether eating hot avocado gives you the runs. For years, we've heard people warn never to order avocado on that quesadilla from your favorite food truck; sage advice or a bullshit wives' tale? Who cares, biting into a hot block of nature's butter is dangerously fun! Test it yourself by quartering

a perfectly ripe avo and dunking it in a standard beer batter (pg. 59). Deep fry in canola oil for about 45 seconds or until batter turns a crispy, light brown. Salt and sprinkle with dried cilantro, onion powder, a squirt of lemon, and minced jalapeño (or your favorite dry spice mix) and fold this hot guac fry into a warm corn tortilla. But stay close to home an hour after, just in case.

ⓥ Mushroom Ceviche

Serves 12

Fungi have always been our faux-meat weapon of choice. When we're not contorting oyster mushrooms into fried po' boy sandwiches (pg. 68) or grinding roasted shitakes into burger patties (pg. 55) we just laze about, gnawing on our tempeh pacifiers and crying little rivers of TVP tears. Seriously though, mushrooms are one of the most versatile regulars in our fridges and we're always trying new ways to utilize their awesome, mysterious glory. This recipe is a bit of a hack job on one of our mentors, the inimitable Father Votar of Elf Cafe. For a birthday party a few years back he made such a ripping mushroom ceviche that we've fiendishly stalked his idea through countless citrus-soaked imitations (white beans the size of clams, all-raw versions versus all-roasted versions) until we found one that finally stomps the master. A combo of dainty lime cured shrooms and their larger, lightly roasted relatives sings with textural conundrums and screams for fresh chips and guac, or just a warm tortilla and some hot sauce. Sorry boss.

4–6 king oyster mushrooms
8 ounces oyster mushrooms
8 ounces white beech
    mushrooms
8 ounces brown beech
    mushrooms
8 ounces crimini mushrooms
1 bunch radishes
1 bunch cilantro
2 jalapeños
2 red Fresno Chiles
Canola spray

LECHE DEL TIGRE MARINADE
1 ½ cups lime juice
    (about 10 limes)
1 cup olive oil
3 teaspoons sea salt
2 red onions, diced

Beverage

Firestone
Walker,
Pale 31

Soundtrack

"Los Angeles,"
Frank Black

////////////

HEY YOU!

Don't even think about using bottled lime juice here. You're making a classic citrus marinade the Peruvians call "tiger's milk." Take pride.

////////////

1. Select 350 on your oven.

2. Juice all them limes and combine in a mixing bowl with olive oil and salt. Whisk. It. Good. Then add the diced onions and let sit.

3. Place your chiles on top of your stove top burner and turn the flame to high. Let 'em sit on the fire for 3 to 5 minutes and then turn them with tongs to expose each of their sides to the flame. You're shooting for solid black all over; don't be afraid to burn. When blackened, place the chiles in a paper bag, crimp it, and let 'em sit.

4. Tear the oyster mushrooms. For the kings, trim their woody ends and then slice in half down the middle lengthwise, then turn and slice both pieces into a handful of thick half-moons. Place oysters on one side of a sheet pan and king oysters on the other, spray with canola oil, and lightly toss to coat. Shove it in the oven for 15 to 20 minutes, or until the kings get some color and the oysters get crispy around the gills.

5. Trim the ends off the brown and white beech mushrooms and slice in half. Trim the ends of the criminis and slice as thinly as your knife skills safely allow. Do the same with the radishes (if you're looking for a real ripping pink, mincing the radishes works even better). Pick the leaves off the entire bunch of cilantro and combine with all of the above in a large mixing bowl.

6. Remove the chiles from their paper knapsack. Rub the charred skin off with your finger tips and discard. (Do not wash, the extra char residue, while probably carcinogenic, tastes good.) Depending on your heat tolerance, seed 1, 2, or all the chiles by gently slicing the outside "walls" of the pepper, and cleaning out the connective membranes and seeds. Add to the mushroom bowl.

7. Dress with the citrus marinade, toss, and check for seasoning adjustment. Then wrap it up and let rest in your fridge for at least 2 hours. Serve with chips, or fresh corn tortillas.

Elote al Echo Parque

Serves 6

Corn on the cob is an essential element to any American cookout, but just like with any and all of our new world produce, the natives do it waaaay better than we invaders. In Echo Park and many other spots in LA, short, stout grannies from Oaxaca peddle fire-cooked, freshly shucked ears of corn smothered with hot sauce, mayo, and parm from a can. It's a vivid and addictive street snack that would make Alex's Grandpa—a notable grump—giggle. (OK, he was kind of a jerk, but damn did the man grow sweet corn.) Yeah, we've made a few modifications that not so discreetly push this snack into the world of AmAp-bedecked young professionals, but it still has a Ghetto Fab vibe. And while Pecorino Romano may not be nearly as street glam as one of those heartless green cans of shake-parm, we only buy Sini Fulvi's wheels, which definitely qualify as OG, since they're the only Pecorino Romano being produced anywhere near Rome.

6 ears of corn, unhusked
6 tablespoons labneh or
    mayonnaise
6 teaspoons Maldon salt

6 teaspoons urfa biber
6 ounces Pecorino Romano
1 lime
½ cup cilantro leaves

1. Well, you have to have a grill going.

2. Toss the unshucked ears of corn on the grill and cap it. Give them a quarter turn every 5 minutes until the outer husk is dry and toasted. This could as long as 20 minutes depending on where your coals are. Remove the ears and let cool.

3. Grate the Pecorino on a microplane or the smallest hole on your box grater. Divide that lime into six equal wedges. Mince the cilantro.

4. Peel away the outer layers of the husk and remove as much silk as you can with your hands. Then hold the corn close over an open flame, or place back on top of the grill to burn off extra silk. Leave the cobs on the grill, or continue to toast turn over an open flame on your stove-top until 60 to 70 percent of the kernels have browned slightly.

5. Assemble each cob one at a time and hand them off immediately: start by rubbing an ear of corn with a section of lime. Then, using a spatula, cover all the kernels liberally with labneh or mayo. Sprinkle on the salt, the urfa, the cilantro, and then finish by adhering as much Pecorino as possible to whatever remaining wet spots remain on your cob.

6. Repeat.

Beverage

Eagle Rock,
Populist

Soundtrack

"I Love LA,"
Randy Newman

Pineapple Escabeche Ⓥ

Makes a shitload

1 pineapple
1 white onion
12 jalapeños
6 small carrots
2–3 teaspoons grapeseed oil
2 cups apple cider vinegar
1 cup white vinegar

2 cups filtered water
2 tablespoons kosher salt
2 tablespoons agave (or sugar)
2 cinnamon sticks
4 bay leaves
8 whole cloves
4 sprigs fresh oregano

Beverage

Ballast Point,
Sculpin IPA

Soundtrack

"Spanish
Bombs,"
The Clash

1. Prepare the veggies. Wash the jalapeños, trim their stems, and score them once each by slicing a shallow "x" on one side; wash and peel the carrots then slice each into three or four pieces along the diagonal; peel and slice the onion.

2. Lightly grease a large skillet with grapeseed oil and heat on medium heat. Add the jalapeños and sauté for several minutes, tossing to cook evenly. Once blistered lightly, remove them and reserve in a bowl. Add another drizzle of oil and cook the carrots in a similar fashion, tossing every 20 seconds. Once softening, but before browning, remove carrots to bowl. Finally, turn heat to low, drizzle oil, and cook the onions for 2 to 3

minutes. Once soft but before translucent, remove them to the bowl. Set aside.

3. Slice up the pineapple: cut off the top and the bottom, then slice off the skin by cutting downward then rotating, and repeat. Now, lay the pineapple down lengthwise and cut it into quarters. Take one quarter and eat or store in the fridge for later. Slice another quarter into thick matchsticks and add this to the bowl. Slice the other half into chunks removing the slightly tougher core and discard.

4. Combine the pineapple chunks with 2 cups water in a blender and pulse for at least a minute until uniform, leaving a foamy pine-

continued on following page

Epazote
why you need wormseed

In response, dear friend, to your spoken-out-loud-while-reading-your-new-awesome-cookbook-question: epazote is an awesome esoteric herb that you might never lay your hands on—unless you know to ask. It's a rare find, even in our forever summer wonderland, and even if you locate it, you might find you don't enjoy its bordering-on-toxic flavor. Epazote, also known as wormseed, is traditionally used to season quesadillas, any dish involving huitlacoche, and beans (its widely believed to nullify the legume's ability to make you fart).

With a chemical flavor that hedges between a mash up of all your garden herbs and strong cleaning product, it's also used as a pesticide and will kill any intestinal worms you may have picked up (hence the ugly nickname). The next time you find yourself at a farmers market stand run by a Mexican, ask them if they grow it. If they do, you just won yourself a pass to the cool kids club. Before you know it, your new farmer friend may be plying you with other esoteric herbs that the rest of the Sunday shoppers have never heard of. (Hint: papaloquelite.)

apple juice. Strain this into a measuring cup; you should have about 3 cups. Set aside.

5. In a large saucepan, combine vinegar with spices and heat on high heat. Once nearing a boil, add pineapple juice. Whisk. Add salt and agave and let reach a boil. Meanwhile, place the sautéed veggies in your vessel, and stick the oregano in the sides. Once the vinegar-pineapple brine reaches a boil, carefully pour atop the veggies in a 6-quart vessel. Let cool with the lid loosely affixed for several minutes, then secure the top and refrigerate for at least 4 to 5 days before serving. Stays good for up to 2 weeks.

Sunstroke Salad ⓥ

Serves 6 to 8

2 tablespoons olive oil
2 zucchini
2 yellow summer squash
1 red onion
2 ears of corn
1 teaspoon cumin seeds
1 teaspoon sea salt
8 epazote leaves (optional,
      but see opposite page)
salted water for blanching

1. Fill a medium-sized pot up to its rivets with water, add a rough tablespoon of sea salt, and set to boil uncovered.

2. Slice the zucchini into rounds on a 45-degree bias. Do the same with the yellow squash. Skin and dice the onion. Shuck the corn, and burn off extra silk over an open flame.

3. That water should be hot. Blanch the squash in shifts; no need to ice them, just wait for the surface of that water to begin to move, toss in a handful, wait for the water to move again, remove, and repeat. Julienne the yellow squash, set both aside.

4. Heat a cast-iron skillet or a large sauté pan on high heat. Toss in the corn and the onions. When they start to pop, shake 'em around a bit.

5. After the onions start to stick a little, toss in the cumin seeds and 1 tablespoon of oil. Toss to coat. Now add the squash; all the zucchini first, then the yellow squash, with about 3 minutes of time between the first and second type.

6. Add the epazote leaves. Keep them whole if you and your guests are beginners; mince them for better coverage if you're a veteran. Kill the flames, finish with remaining olive oil and salt, then serve immediately.

 Beverage
Craftsman,
Sour Braggot

 Soundtrack
"Drinkin' and
Blo," Redbone

Ambient Nachos

Serves 6 to 8

We came up with the idea of self-cooking nachos during a July camping trip we took to Ojai, the hippie spa town northwest of LA. We'd hiked down a dry riverbed in 100-degree weather, past a gun range, to find a hidden water hole and stripped to our skivvies. Before diving in, we wanted to get some kind of meal cooking. We were armed simply with fruit, water, nuts, a bag of tortilla chips, and a hunk of cheese in our backpack. The nacho connoisseur among us tore the bag in half, lopped off cheese with a pocket knife, and fangled the foil-lined bag into a science-geek oven to harness the sun. ("Sun Chips" jokes were made.) After we splashed around, our solar snack had melted to gooey perfection. Since that trip we've updated the recipe to include Limburger, which melts in mild temperatures whether you're outside or not, to make the dish truly ambient. Handmade chips with a light garnish of hot chiles, scallions, and urfa biber let it fly. You can either plan ahead by frying chips before you leave or you can use store-bought and forego everything but cheese, chips, and sun.

Beverage

Weihenstephaner, 1809

Soundtrack

"Jesus Built My Hotrod," Ministry

////////////

HEY YOU!

If you ever deep-fry anything, get a spider already. It's that webbed metal fry basket on a long wooden stick. You wanna advance to oyster mushroom po' boys, don't you?

////////////

30 mini corn tortillas
3 cups canola oil for frying
1 tablespoon salt
8 ounces Anton's Bavarian Limburger
4–6 green Thai chiles
3 scallions
1 teaspoon urfa biber

1. If frying your own chips, prepare a fry station. Fill a thick-bottomed pot half way with canola oil and set on high heat. Place a cookie sheet lined with several paper towels next to the stove. While you wait for oil to heat, slice the corn tortillas into half moons. After about 10 minutes, test the oil by dropping a small piece of tortilla in; it should sizzle, float, and brown within 20 seconds.

2. Once oil is hot, begin frying in small batches of about 8 to 10 half-moons by dropping them one at a time (to prevent oil eruptions). Using your spider or metal spatula, press the chips down below the surface several times and carefully flip them after 45 seconds, or once they start to puff and brown lightly. After about 2 minutes they should be done. Fish the chips out and shake gently over the pot to remove excess oil and then deposit onto the towel-lined tray. Repeat until all chips are fried.

3. While still warm sprinkle with sea salt.

4. To assemble ambient nachos: line a cookie sheet with a piece of aluminum foil slightly longer than the pan, so that the excess foil can be bent up about 2 inches toward the sky to capture extra heat. (You can do this without a cookie sheet if necessary, just don't spill.)

5. Distribute chips evenly onto the sheet pan. Remove the Limburger from the refrigerator or cooler, slice into thin squares, and distribute evenly over the chips. Finely mince the chiles and slice the scallions on a diagonal. Sprinkle with urfa biber or add any additional garnish as desired (dry is better than wet). Set out in a sunny place for at least 1 hour. Once the cheese has oozed, it's ready to eat.

Wild Grub

THE FIRST TIME THE TWO OF US WENT CAMPING TOGETHER, IT WAS A TWO-MAN DEATH MISSION. We scaled boulders with bourbon bottles in hand. Our dinner was made up of only peanut butter spread on cold tortillas—until Alex dropped his on the ground facedown: rocks were added as a garnish and he kept eating.

We now **travel fat with provisions** when we go into the wild: spices and dried herbs in zip-lock bags, oils and vinegar bottles strapped in a milk crate, a bevy of pans, and a cooler for produce and beer. This kind of **luxurious campfire cooking** is not for everyone—but not everyone is invited on our camping trips.

When we head for the hills on weekend hikes, we bring the same approach, though not the milk crates or coolers obviously. **Being outdoors surrounded by delicious nature** is hardly an excuse to eat unseasoned hardtack or bad trail mix.

WILD GRUB

Red Haterade Ⓥ

Makes 2 pints

Years of high school punk shows taught us to love red Gatorade, our classic and preferred electrolyte refreshment after being jostled in a mosh pit. The high-fructose corn syrup and red dye, however, we can pass on. We've found bright magenta batches of fruit punch elixir, using sea salt and agave, has almost the same effect.

//////////

HEY YOU!

Hydrate or die trying. Bring extra water on your hike (duh) and dilute your Haterade as you drain it to make it go as far as you can.

//////////

Beverage

You're already drunk

Soundtrack

"Decepticon (DFA remix)" Le Tigre

4 cups filtered water
2 tablespoons flor de Jamaica
    (dried hibiscus)
4 strawberries
6 raspberries
quarter of a pineapple
juice of one orange
1 tablespoon lemon juice
1 teaspoon kosher salt
4 tablespoons agave syrup

1. Bring 4 cups of filtered water to a boil. Measure out the Jamaica and add to a large bowl or other vessel. Once boiling, pour the water onto the Jamaica. Let sit for 20 minutes, until dark red and room temperature. Strain through a fine mesh strainer into a large mixing bowl.

2. Carve off about 3 1-inch thick slices of peeled pineapple, chop into cubes and measure; there should be about 1 cup. Put the fruit in a blender. Add the berries and puree for several minutes until frothy. Pour the puree through a fine mesh strainer, making sure to remove any seeds or fruit chunks. Re-strain if necessary.

3. Slowly add the strained fruit mixture to the mixing bowl with the pink tea. Whisk the mixture and as you do, slowly add the agave, followed by the salt. Pour lemon and orange juice through a strainer to prevent pulp. Store in a bottle with a lid and keep refrigerated. Taste and dilute with filtered water if too sweet for you (about half a cup is perfect but will dilute the color).

Summer Seitan ⓥ

Makes 1 loaf

Seitan can be a versatile outdoor snack, since it's part-bread, part-fake meat and travels better than both. Bring along a loaf for grilling at a campsite, or better yet pack seitan banh mi sandwiches for day trips. Like a lot of things that require broth, seitan can be as weak or as strong as the stock you use to make it. Bouillon is serviceable; a broth from home kitchen scraps is better; but what if we built upon a full blown soup base? It takes planning, but you weren't going to forgo the Boy Scout motto were you?

SOUP BASE
2 8-ounce cans coconut milk
1 tablespoon grapeseed oil
3 stalks lemongrass
5 cloves garlic, minced
¼ cup fresh ginger, minced
4-6 Thai chiles
1 tablespoon white miso paste
1 cup filtered water
juice of one lime
1 ½ teaspoons turmeric
sea salt to taste

SEITAN MIX
3 cups gluten flour
1 cup pastry flour
4 cups soup base
2 tablespoons coriander seed
2 tablespoons fresh cracked black pepper

//////////

HEY YOU!

This carbo load is best in a sandwich after a good searing. Chill it down in your fridge and slice it thin, then sear in a hot pan with oil until its crispy.

//////////

1. Start the soup the night before you want to bake seitan: slam the lemongrass on your cutting board several times to release its oils, then cut each stalk into four or so 3-inch pieces. Put a medium-sized stock pot onto medium heat with the grapeseed oil. Add the lemongrass stalks followed by the minced ginger, then sauté for 2 or 3 minutes. Roughly chop the chiles and add to the pot, seeds and all. Add the garlic, stir, and cook for another 2. Finally add turmeric and toast for 30 seconds before dousing it all in coconut milk. Blend miso into the water, and combine with the coconut broth.

2. Once bubbling, set to simmer, giving it a quick stir every 30 seconds and cook for 5 minutes. Turn it off, squeeze the fresh lime, top it with a lid, and let it sit for at least 2 hours before using. (Or stick it in the fridge overnight.)

3. When ready to cook, preheat oven to 375 degrees. (If you left it in the fridge overnight, remove the coconut soup for 30 minutes or so to take off the chill.) Combine the two flours in a mixing bowl. Toast the coriander seeds over medium heat until fragrant, about

4 minutes, and remove, tossing to keep from burning. Crush with a knife or in a mortar and pestle and add to the flour.

4. Over a separate bowl, strain the soup to remove all the chunks, spices, and stalks, leaving just a yellow cream.

5. Combine half the soup with the flour and mix with a spatula, then slowly add more until it forms a consistent gooey dough that's moist but not wet. You should have used all the soup or all but a couple tablespoons. Line a bread pan with wax paper, spray it well with canola oil, and slide the seitan dough in. Drizzle more oil on top of the dough and add a ton of fresh cracked black pepper before capping with aluminum foil. Lastly, create a double boiler by placing this pan inside a larger casserole dish filled halfway with water and stick the whole shebang in the oven.

6. Cook for 1 hour and 45 minutes, rotating halfway through. Ten minutes before removing, take off the foil (it should still be slightly doughy in the center) and cook uncovered. Carefully remove the seitan loaf from its pan and set on cooling rack or a cutting board.

Beverage

Sierra Nevada, Foam

Soundtrack

"Sky Holds the Sun," Band of Bees

Backpack ⓥ Banh Mi

HEY YOU!

Seal these
sandwiches up in
plastic wrap and
let em sit for up
to 5 hours before
you eat em. Sous
vide in the wild!

/////////

Beverage

Oskar Blues,
Old Chub

Soundtrack

"Damaged
Goods,"
Gang of Four

Makes 6

2 baguettes
half a seitan loaf (pg. 30)
⅛ cup grapeseed oil for frying
1 cup pickled daikon and carrots (next page)
1 cup cilantro stems
4 tablespoons veganaise
2 tablespoons Sriracha
2 tablespoons hoisin (next page)
2 jalapeños

1. Slice open the baguettes with a serrated knife, leaving the top and bottom attached. Slather the top of the baguette with Sriracha and the bottom with veganaise.

2. Heat a wide sauté pan on medium-high heat while you slice off pieces of seitan just slightly thicker than most deli meats. Add a tablespoon of oil to the pan and sauté as many seitan slices as you can fit without overlapping.

Cook for 2 to 3 minutes on one side, or until brown, and then flip, being careful not to let them stick or tear. As they finish, arrange them evenly on the baguette.

3. Finally add your pickled daikon and carrot, fresh cilantro stems, and jalapeño slices (cut on a bias). Cut each baguette into three pieces, each about 5 inches long.

Banh Mi Pickles ⓥ

Makes enough for a week

- 1 medium daikon radish
- 3–4 large carrots
- 1 cup filtered water
- ¾ cup white vinegar
- ¼ cup rice wine vinegar
- ¼ cup white sugar
- 2 tablespoons sea salt

1. Peel and wash the daikon and carrots. Slice them into even matchsticks about 4 inches long and as thin as you can make them.

2. Place matchsticks in a mixing bowl and sprinkle with salt. Using both hands, scrunch the veggies gently to massage the salt into them, drawing out their water. Do this for about a minute, until light orange juice collects in the bowl and the matchsticks turn slightly limp.

3. Combine vinegars, sugar, and water in a saucepan on medium heat. Whisk to combine and let it hit a boil, turning it down to a simmer. Cook for 3 minutes then remove from heat.

4. Cram the veggies in an 18-ounce jar. Cover with brine and top with a lid. Let cool on the counter for 30 minutes, then fridge 'em for at least a day. They last as long as 2 weeks.

Hoisin ⓥ

Makes about a cup

- ½ cup soy sauce
- ¼ cup rice vinegar
- ¼ cup cider vinegar
- 3 garlic cloves, minced
- a pinch of cinnamon
- 3 ripe plums, chopped
- 5 tablespoons agave syrup
- 1 tablespoon vegetable oil
- ½ teaspoon sesame oil
- 1 teaspoon fresh cracked
  black pepper

1. Combine two of the chopped plums, oils, vinegars, and agave in a small saucepan on medium heat. Once you hit a boil, lower to simmer and add all the rest of the ingredients except soy sauce and the third plum. Cook for 10 minutes, or until reduced slightly and plums fall apart.

2. Now add the soy, and let it cook for another 5 minutes. Remove and cool.

3. Pulse all this well in a blender, adding the third plum raw as you blend. Once creamy, push through a fine mesh strainer to remove any debris. Refrigerate to firm up.

Bahn Mi Pickles

Beverage
Green Flash,
Double Stout

"Amanaemonesia,"
Chairlift

Hoisin

Beverage
St. Sebastiaan,
Yeast Hoist

Soundtrack
"The Wanderer,"
U2 Featuring
Johnny Cash

Butter Beer Flapjacks

Makes 8 to 10

Beverage

Goose Island, Bourbon County Stout

Soundtrack

"I'm So Free," Lou Reed

Waking up when the days are long means breakfast comes early. What's both easy and sustaining? Ale-carbonated flapjacks are the answer, whether you're making a campfire breakfast in a National Forest or just a Sunday patio brunch after a group sleep-over. Toppings can vary from sweet (nuts, syrups, fruits) to savory (caramelized onions, greens, cheese). If you're caught in the wilderness without a cooler for the buttermilk, here's a tip: buy buttermilk powder at any good health foods store and sub a quarter of a cup with water.

3 cups all-purpose flour
1 cup cornmeal
4 teaspoons baking powder
1 stick melted butter plus ½ stick extra
2 cups buttermilk
1 cup pale ale
4 organic eggs (about 1 cup)

1. Mix dry ingredients in a large bowl. Pour and measure beer, allowing foam to subside. Measure out the eggs, beat them, and combine them with all other wet ingredients in a second mixing bowl. Stir well.

2. Pour the wet ingredients into the dry and gently mix just until they're combined (don't go overboard on the whisking).

3. Heat a large skillet or cast-iron over a flame (be it a campfire, camping stove, or normal stovetop). Once the pan is hot, grease it with an extra pad of butter, or some oil. Pour one large flapjack at a time. Let it cook for about 90 seconds or until the bubbling permeates the uncooked side and the underside starts to brown.

4. Carefully place spices and toppings into the flapjack's exposed side before flipping. Cook until the bottom is evenly brown. (If there's a topping, you want to lightly caramelize whatever it is.) Serve with extra butter and maple syrup.

Camping Stock

how to pack your pantry

Most meals around a campfire revolve around a slow simmer, to ensure you have time to sit around on rocks taking slugs of whisky and properly shoot the shit. Whether it's soup, chili, or a pot of beans, the key overlooked ingredient is liquid, because no matter how fresh that nearby stream may be, cooking anything in boring-ass water is negating everything you've learned in a kitchen. That's why we tuck a baggie of dry-stock fixings into our hiking boots when we hit the trails. The lightest way to pack flavor is dehydrated shrooms, which'll imbue any water with meatiness. Here's the recipe for our go-to mix: 1 ounce dried porcinis, 4 bay leaves, 2 tablespoons smoked paprika, 1 tablespoon ground cumin, 1 tablespoon smoked salt, 1 tablespoon kosher salt, 1 teaspoon cayenne pepper, 1 teaspoon dry cocoa powder.

Hobo Franks & Beans

Serves 4

When the sun sinks, the desert gets surprisingly cold. This minimalist chow has served us well on more than one frigid desert night while we're cutting onions with fingerless gloves and huddling around the stove to keep the burner from being blown out. A little preparty planning (steam wieners before leaving, check; pack your stock spice mix, got it) means you have to do very little to eat well beside your tent. Everything on this list can survive a day of hot hiking without any spoilage—just don't let the bears or coyotes smell your wieners.

- 2 tablespoons olive oil
- 1 onion
- 2 cloves garlic
- 1 15-ounce can black beans
- 1 15-ounce can garbanzo beans
- 4 wieners (pg. 54)
- 2 poblano or bell peppers
- 1 cup camping stock spice-mix (pg. 33)
- 1 ½ cups water

1. Set up a camping stove. Place a pot on high heat and add half the oil. Peel and chop the onion and add half this to the pot and cook for 2 minutes while stirring. Cut the wieners into bite-sized chunks and add. Sauté like this until wieners get brown and slightly crisp. Remove onto a plate and set aside.

2. Wipe pot clean with a rag and put back on the stove with remaining oil. Chop the peppers, mince the garlic, and add them with remaining onions, cook and stir.

3. Once onions are turning translucent but peppers are still slightly crunchy, add the stock spice, and toast for 30 seconds, followed by the water. Open the cans of beans, and drain them too. Cover and cook like this for about 8 to 10 minutes or until the liquid has reduced and you're left with a thick chili of beans.

4. Top the chili with sautéed franks. Serve with tortillas.

HEY YOU!

Wanna take the Hobo Factor up a napsack? Substitute porter for water and you've got the HK caveman special: canned beans and beer.

Beverage

Deschutes, Black Butte Porter

Soundtrack

"Ballad of Jim Jones," Brian Jonestown Massacre

WILD GRUB

Fanny Pack
Popcorn

GOURMANDS AND BIG EATERS ARE SCREWED when it comes to hiking meals, because space (and shoulder strength) comes at a premium. Well-conceived popping corn is the perfect trail fix. Whatever spices, herbs, oils, and salts you decide to flavor these kernels with, follow these basic steps for making flavor cling to the corns.

1. Grind and combine desired spice mix.

2. Place a large soup pot with a lid (preferably a clear lid) on medium-high heat. Add corn kernels and nearly cover them with your oil of choice, either grapeseed, canola, or vegetable (about ⅛ cup). Cap the pot with lid and wait for fireworks. Lay out a sheet pan for tossing with your spice mix later.

3. Corn should start popping within a minute. Once it does, turn down to medium heat and shake the pot every 30 seconds or so. Once the popping dies down, about 3 minutes, turn off the heat.

4. Mix with spices and eat immediately or hours later. (Keeps best if cooled for 5 to 10 minutes to room temp and packed snugly in a Ziplock bag.)

Chile-Cheese

Makes a large bag

- ¼ cup popcorn kernels
- ⅛ cup vegetable oil
- 2 tablespoons buttermilk powder
- 2 tablespoons Parmesan (finely grated)
- 1 tablespoon dried red chile
- 1 teaspoon turmeric, ground
- 1 teaspoon sea salt

Five-Spice Ⓥ

Makes a large bag

- ¼ cup popcorn kernels
- ⅛ cup vegetable oil
- ½ teaspoon sesame oil
- 2 tablespoons star anise, ground
- 1 tablespoon dried red chile
- 1 tablespoon dried ginger, ground
- 1 teaspoon clove, ground
- ½ teaspoon Vietnamese cinnamon, ground
- 1 teaspoon sea salt

Greek Salad Ⓥ

Makes a large bag

- ¼ cup popcorn kernels
- ⅛ cup vegetable oil
- 1 tablespoons dried mint, ground
- 2 tablespoons sumac, ground
- 2 tablespoons za'atar, ground
- 1 teaspoon sea salt

Pizza

Makes a large bag

- ¼ cup popcorn kernels
- ⅛ cup vegetable oil
- 1 tablespoon dried garlic, ground
- 1 tablespoon onion powder
- 1 tablespoon dried red chile flakes, ground
- 1 tablespoon Parmesan, finely grated
- 1 teaspoon fennel seed ground
- 1 teaspoon paprika
- 1 teaspoon sea salt

Guacamole

Makes a large bag

- ¼ cup popcorn kernels
- ⅛ cup vegetable oil
- 2 tablespoons dried cilantro, ground
- 2 tablespoons Parmesan, finely grated
- 1 tablespoon dried red chile
- 1 teaspoon dried lime zest, ground
- 1 teaspoon jalapeño powder (cayenne works)
- 1 teaspoon sea salt

Grass Crackers Ⓥ

Makes about 24

HEY YOU!

Cheese for the trail in two sentences or less?! Ask your monger for mountain cheeses, clothbound cheddars, or grab a washed rind goo-er and see how we conceived our Ambient Nachos.

Beverage

Ommegang, Hennepin

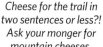

Soundtrack

"Sun Shadow Drifter," White Rainbow

If Alex had his way crackers would be banned from most cheese spreads, allowing only fruits, fingers, and pocket knives, and leaving all the more attention (and stomach space) for animal fats. But baking your own crackers is an acceptable exception. These yeasty, wild onion-scented crackers look the part out in the bush with green blades of chives peeking through the surface. And (yes, Alex, it's true) they're a great canvas for cultured milk fat.

1 ½ cup all-purpose flour, plus extra for kneading
¼ cup fresh chives, chopped into long grass-like pieces
1 tablespoon olive oil, plus extra for greasing
1 tablespoon honey (agave works)
½ teaspoon salt
½ teaspoon yeast
⅔ cup water
1 teaspoon urfa biber (black pepper works)
1 tablespoon cracked black pepper

1. In a mixing bowl, combine flour, salt, and yeast. Add the herbs and stir with your hands. In four increments add the water and the honey (or agave), and mush the mixture together. You may not need the last addition of water (you want a ball that sticks together in your palms when pressed, but not so tacky that it sticks to them).

2. On a cutting board dusted with extra flour, knead the dough firmly for about 5 minutes, adding more flour as needed to keep from sticking, then rest the dough. Wash and dry the mixing bowl you used. Take the dough and knead for another 5 minutes, or until smooth and pliable.

3. Drizzle oil around the side of the bowl, bunch the dough together in a rotund ball, and roll it around the oiled bowl. Cover with plastic wrap and sit in a warm place for 90 minutes to 2 hours.

4. When ball has doubled in size, preheat the oven to 350 degrees. On your cutting board, gently tease the dough out with your hands to form a rectangle, and then flatten with a roll-ing pin. Roll firmly for several minutes until the dough is about a centimeter thick and forms a long rectangle to fit a 12 x 18-inch sheet pan. Now spray your pan, sprinkle with corn meal and carefully move dough to the pan. Sprinkle with urfa (or cracked black pepper).

5. Cut desired shapes with a knife (we like squares for cheese and stubby rectangles for backpack snacking). Dough should only slightly bounce back. Bake in the oven for about 12 to 15 minutes or until the sides start to lightly brown. Some puffing is fine. Re-move and let crackers cool before eating or packing. Sprinkle with cracked black pepper.

Power Bars

Peanut Butter, Banana & Pickle

12 dates
½ cup flax seeds
½ cup oats
3 tablespoons peanut butter
   (chunky, salted)
2 tablespoons chopped
   dill pickles (or capers)
1 tablespoon agave or honey
1 banana
½ cup filtered water
Canola spray

Aztec Trailmix

12 dates
½ cup flax seeds
½ cup oats
2 tablespoons cocoa powder
2 tablespoons dried coconut
   (fine)
1 tablespoon agave or honey
1 tablespoon dried red chile
2 tablespoons sesame seeds
zest of one orange
½ cup filtered water
Canola spray

1. The night before (or at least 6 hours before) soak the flax in about ½ cup water, cover, and let sit out on the counter.

2. After the flax has soaked, prepare the rest of the ingredients. Spray a baking sheet with canola oil, spread out the oats, and spray the top. Toast these in a 325 degree oven for about 20 minutes, stirring often to cook evenly. Once lightly brown, remove the oats and let sit to cool for 10 minutes.

3. Meanwhile, pit the dates and pulse in a food processor until you have a gooey ball of date puree. In a bowl combine the flax seeds (which should be like glue) and the date puree. Using a fork, mash the two together to form a thick seed paste.

4. Add all the remaining ingredients except the oats and the sesame (in the case of Aztec trailmix) or banana (in the case of the peanut butter, banana, and pickle). Mix well.

5. Lastly, add the oats, stirring just enough to thoroughly combine; don't stir too much or you'll denature the oats.

6. Preheat oven to 325 degrees and grease a baking sheet again and spoon out the mixture evenly. Using a spatula, form a rectangle out of mixture (about 3 x 10 inches). Smooth it out. Top with either the sesame seeds or thin slices of banana gently pressed into the top.

7. Bake for 20 minutes. Spray the top of your bar block with canola oil, then gently flip to cook the other side. Bake another 10 minutes, then remove and lot cool before cutting into 2 x 4-inch blocks. Let cool, and keep your bars dry until you eat them.

Beverage
Stone,
Ruination

Soundtrack
"Clay Stones,"
We Are the
World

Pizza Pool Party

WE DIG REGIONAL SPECIFICITY. We're into bicoastal hip-hop rivalries. But we're soooo over the yawnfest of the American Pizza Civil War between east and west. Triangular folds of dough and cheese should alleviate conflict, not cause it. Bitch about pizza and you piss on fun itself. **Don't piss on fun, friends.**

So consider this our olive branch: make your pizza yourself, in the least anal way possible: **Throw. It. On. The. Grill.** Forget the bagel-crusted hippie pies of Venice Beach, the floppy, grease-slicked slices the size of a flannel shirt that you get for a dollar in Brooklyn, the indefinable depth of Chicago. Forget the new school of Pizza Nazis peppered all over America that put more stress on their "process" than Tony Bourdain grumbles about vegan assassins slitting his throat. Remember instead that **pizza equals party.** It should be chilled out, awesome, and paired with beer. Follow us toward that achievable goal, pizza fiends: **have a piece, make peace.**

Ale Dough Ⓥ

Makes 6 pies

/////////

HEY YOU!

Why would we ever tell you to put ice in your IPA? Because this ain't for drinking, we're baking here and we want our baking beer colder than the Rockies.

/////////

The first pizzas we ever made were based on a cuban bread recipe; we used porter instead of water, too much yeast, and cooked 'em way too long at way too low a temperature. They were dense carb-and-cheese bombs that knocked us flatter than the gravity bong rips we took before going to World Politics 101. This mother dough is a formula that oscillates between our pre–Hot Knives cooking habits and our post–Peter Reinhart school of hard-assed home bread-ery. (If you haven't read Reinhart's *The Bread Baker's Apprentice* get thee to the library). Proper technique, suffused with our pathological need to put beer in everything, has made this dough much better than it was in 2004.

Beverage
Stone,
Levitation Ale

Soundtrack
"Kracked,"
Dinosaur Jr.

1 ½ cups all-purpose flour
½ teaspoon instant yeast
¾ teaspoon salt
½ cup plus ⅓ cup IPA
¼ cup olive oil

1. Measure out your beer and then add ice cubes to it.

2. Combine dry goods in a mixing bowl with your hands.

3. Add the olive oil and the beer—not the ice—to the dry goods and stir to combine with a wooden spoon, or your hand, until all the ingredients have glommed together in a big sticky ball. Transfer said ball onto a floured work surface and knead it for 10 minutes.

4. Pat the dough into a log. Cut it in half, then the half in thirds. Roll each lump into a ball with your hands. Splash a little olive oil in a mixing bowl, then roll each ball in olive oil to coat. Wrap 'em in plastic, then let them live in your fridge overnight. These can be frozen for a few weeks as well.

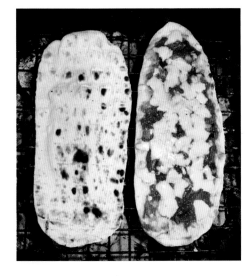

Pool Crust
roll, grill and flip your slice

Remove your dough balls from the fridge about an hour before you plan to use them (if frozen, thaw overnight). Unwrap them and stage them on a parchment-lined sheet pan. Now, get that grill hot as hell and clean as heaven. Make sure that you've got all your toppings ready, because you'll have a very short window when the grilling begins. Roll out a dough ball on a floured surface as thin as possible. Sometimes it's better to make them oblong so you can fit two on the grill at a time. Gently lay the dough across the grill and cap it immediately. Count to 30—or quickly roll out another ball of dough—then flip the dough and cap the grill. Thirty seconds later, remove the now-crust (mostly firm but not yet browned) and splatter at will with any and all toppings. Place back on the grill for about 2 minutes, or as long as it takes for cheese to melt, toppings to get hot, and the bottom of the crust to char a little. Repeat with reckless abandon.

Pea Pod Pesto ⓥ

Makes enough for 3 pies

1 cup almonds, raw
2 cups English peas, in pods
3 garlic cloves
¾ cup extra virgin olive oil
2 teaspoons white wine vinegar

2 tablespoons flat-leaf parsley
1 tablespoon kosher salt,
   for blanching
sea salt and fresh black pepper
   to taste

1. Start by blanching the almonds. Heat a few cups of water in a tea kettle and place the nuts in large bowl. Once boiling, dump water over the nuts and let sit for 2 minutes before draining and covering with cool water. Once cooled, simply grab a nut and pop off its skin by applying pressure to one end-point. Discard skins.

2. Shell and blanch the peas. Fill a pot with water, add kosher salt, and place it back on high heat. Make an ice bath. Prepare the pea pods by snapping the tip of each pod and pulling the stringy thread downward. Discard the string; reserve the peas for later use; use the pod only for making the pesto. Once water hits a boil, dump in the pea pods and cook for 30 seconds. Strain them out and dunk in ice bath for several minutes.

3. Add two-thirds of the blanched pods to a food processor (saving the rest for later) along with the peeled garlic cloves and two-thirds of the blanched almonds. Pulse for 1 minute while slowly adding all but a tablespoon of the olive oil, followed by all the vinegar. Stop once creamy and remove the pesto to a mixing bowl.

4. With a knife, finely chop the remaining pea pods and blanched almonds, as well as the flat-leaf parsley. Combine and stir with the remaining tablespoon of olive oil. Season to taste and serve at room temperature.

Beverage

Ladyface,
Workers
Cohopritive

Soundtrack

"Six Pack,"
Black Flag

Porcini Porcine ⓥ

Makes enough for 3 pies

½ cup dried porcini
    mushrooms (whole,
    flat pieces)
2–3 candy-stripe beets
½ cup warm water
1 teaspoon sea salt
½ teaspoon liquid smoke
2 teaspoons grain mustard

Beverage

Bear Republic,
Hop Rod Rye

Soundtrack

"Bacon Fat,"
Taj Mahal

1. Carefully peel the beets. (You want to see some bright pink stripes, otherwise the color won't work.) Pulse beets in a blender along with enough warm water to make them move, between ⅓ and ½ cup. Strain this over fine mesh into a bowl to leave only juice.

2. Combine the pink beet juice with sea salt, liquid smoke, and mustard and whisk. Then place the dried porcinis in a container with a lid, and pour the juice-brine over them. It should be enough to cover them completely. Let soak at least 20 minutes before using.

Grilled Marinara Ⓥ

Makes enough for 6 pies

4 medium tomatoes
  (we prefer Momotoros)
¼ cup of olive oil
4 cloves of garlic
⅛ cup of picked oregano leaves
1 teaspoon salt
2 teaspoons ground black pepper

1. Roast the tomatoes whole over coals until they are practically falling apart. Rotate them after 10 to 15 minutes to make sure that each side is exposed to direct heat. Once they start bursting and losing juice into the flames, they are done. Trim what's left of stems off and let the tomatoes rest for a moment.

2. Peel and crush the garlic. Combine oil, tomatoes, garlic, salt, and oregano in a blender and puree until smooth. Dress pizzas. Leftovers make for awesome pasta sauce, punchy Bloody Mary base, or the beginnings of ripping salsa.

Beverage

Maui Brewing,
Flyin' HI.P.Hay

Soundtrack

"Barcelona,"
The Rentals

Beer Cheese

BEER AND CHEESE (ARGUABLY OUR TWO FAVORITE FOOD GROUPS) ARE RARELY COMBINED IN A MANNER THAT SUITS EITHER. With the exception of a seasonal oozer called Winnamere from Jasper Hills Farms, which is washed in real lambic and tastes like eating bacon while running through a pine forest, most "beer cheeses" are step-down cheddars with low-end hops thrown in. Or marbled monstrosities that taste like cake. Taking a cue from the new school of using food additives to achieve unheard of textural results, we riffed on a technique typically used to make the un-meltable melt. Sodium citrate (a semi-naturally derived technical salt) keeps the fat and the lactic solids from separating, which means you can use this basic recipe with any cheese you would otherwise never get gooey on pizza or burgers, like Parmigiano or a hard-ass, bandage-wrapped cheddar. The result is a very workable (i.e., it melts fast) "processed" cheese that's 30 percent beer. Don't try making this with super hoppy, bitter beers. Use yeast-forward golden ales, or try it with porters or low hopped stouts. As science-y as it sounds, you can buy sodium citrate from any good gourmet food store, or just order it online.

Pizza Cheese

Makes enough for 6 pies

- 1 cup Belgian golden ale
- 8 ounces Pecorino Romano, grated
- 8 ounces Gruyère, grated
- ½ ounce sodium citrate
- 2 teaspoons black pepper
- 4 cloves garlic smashed
- 12 leaves fresh oregano (or 2 teaspoons dry)

1. Combine beer and spices (not the sodium citrate) in a small saucepan on medium heat. When it hits a boil, cut the heat and let sit to infuse for 10 more minutes. Strain out the solids and discard them; save the liquid.

2. Return the liquid to the heat and add the sodium citrate. Whisk until it's all dissolved. Now gradually add the cheese in small amounts—like ⅛ cup at a time—waiting to add more until the previous amount melts into the beer. After all the cheese is melted, cool it down and let it recoagulate into a beer-and-cheese frankenmonster.

3. Shape depending on use. For burger slices: line a baking sheet with a silpat or parchment paper and pour the melted cheese on the tray and let cool for 1 hour. Cut into squares or any other shapes you like. Store slices with wax paper betwixt each in the fridge. For grating on pizzas (or anything else): dump the cheese mix into a breadpan, a ramekin, or any such vessel and chill that fucker out in the fridge. Grate at will.

Burger Cheese

Makes enough for 8 burgers

(see above for instructions)

- ½ cup Belgian Golden Ale
- 8 ounces Gruyère, grated
- ¼ ounce sodium citrate
- 6 black peppercorns
- 6 white peppercorns
- 1 teaspoon salt
- 2 garlic cloves, peeled and smashed

Eggplant Crasserole

Serves 8

The comically plump and shiny globe eggplants are not as cute once you get them home and don't know what to cook. Suddenly they're baffling, dry, ogre vegetables that get passed over for easier salad veg all week long. For help, look no further than the salt jar and your faucet: sitting eggplant steaks in a spiced brine makes them tender straight off the skillet or grill, battered and fried. A casserole of brined eggplant parm is a fitting summer tribute. Here, we take a ratatouille approach.

FENNEL BRINE
6 cups filtered water
¾ cup balsamic vinegar
2 tablespoons fennel seed
    (ground)
2 tablespoons kosher salt
1 tablespoon honey
2 globe eggplants

2 organic eggs
1 ½ cups all-purpose flour
2 cups breadcrumbs
    (finely ground)
1 ½ cup grapeseed oil
    (for frying)
3 tablespoons olive oil
3 tablespoons balsamic
    vinegar
4 ripe tomatoes
1 red onion
2 sprigs fresh oregano
2 ounces pizza cheese (pg. 46)
sea salt to taste

Beverage

La Chouffe,
Houblon

Soundtrack

"Outta My
System," My
Morning Jacket

1. The day before, brine the eggplant. Prepare the brine in a 4-liter container with a lid. Fill container with vinegar, salt, ground fennel seed, and honey. Bring the water to a boil and pour it in too. Whisk thoroughly.

2. Cut off the tips of the eggplants and slice each of them into several 1-centimeter-thick steaks. Wedge them into the container of brine so that there is some space in between each piece. To keep them submerged, top with a small ceramic plate or a plastic bag filled with additional water. Cover with the lid and refrigerate like this overnight (or as long as 2 days).

/////////// **The Next Day** ///////////

3. Remove eggplants from the brine, shake off, and let sit in a colander to dry. Prepare a

batter station with three widemouth bowls: flour in one, beaten egg in the next, and bread crumbs in the third. Season the flour with salt and pepper. Have a clean baking sheet ready to sit the battered eggplant.

4. Batter two eggplant steaks at a time: pat them in flour until covered, shaking excess flour off. Then dip them in the egg wash, letting excess egg drip off.

Place each steak into the breadcrumbs. Bury them to coat completely and gently set aside on tray. Repeat until done, adding more flour, egg, breadcrumbs as needed.

5. To fry, add enough grapeseed oil to a wide pan or cast-iron so it covers the surface about a centimeter deep. Once hot, drop two or three eggplant steaks into the oil.

continued on following page

continued on following page

HEY YOU!

When composing this hodgepodge casserole, be artistic but don't be afraid to jam veggies every which way until the dish is snug.

(It should sizzle.) Gently apply weight with a spatula for the first 20 seconds. Once browning, flip carefully so you don't lose breading. When brown on the second side, remove and let sit on a paper towel. Repeat until done.

6. Slice the tomato and onion into rounds about half a centimeter-thick. Preheat the oven to 375 degrees and assemble your casserole. Grease the dish with half the olive oil. Carefully lay half the fried eggplant down, so the steaks are barely touching. Top each steak with an onion and tomato slice. Sprinkle with sea salt. Then top with another layer of eggplant. Arrange all of this this such that there are cracks in between, then stuff more tomato and onion slices vertically into these cracks. Sprinkle again with salt. Drizzle remaining olive oil on top.

7. Cover the casserole dish with aluminum foil and slide it into the oven. Bake for about 30 to 35 minutes. Once you hear the vegetables sizzling go ahead and remove the foil, pull the dish out just enough to drizzle with the additional 3 tablespoons of balsamic vinegar. Return to the oven for 8 to 10 minutes.

8. Remove and top with pizza cheese and fresh oregano leaves, let rest for 5 minutes, and serve.

Pizza Salad

Beverage

Telegraph, Reserve Wheat

Soundtrack

"The Swimming Song," Loudon Wainright III

Serves 4

To Italians, panzanella may be a great-great-grandmotherly culinary tradition from one of their most respected regions and with deeply felt connections to their identity—but to us, it's pizza as a salad! Don't take that the wrong way, we think pizza as a salad is downright fucking brilliant, there's just no point to putting it on some kind of rustic, handcrafted pedestal. It's old bread in warm tomato juices tossed with stuff. And it's the best thing to happen to salad since taco salad.

3 bolillo rolls, one-day old (or 1 baguette)
3 tablespoons extra virgin olive oil
3 teaspoons balsamic vinegar
2 teaspoons sea salt
12 caper berries
half a red onion, peeled
2 red bell peppers
¾ cup tomato vinaigrette (pg. 94)
¼ cup Italian parsley
a sprig of fresh oregano
a sprig of lemon basil

1. Prepare your slightly stale bolillos for grilling. Drizzle the olive oil on a large plate, followed by the balsamic, making sure to distribute evenly, and sprinkle with 1 teaspoon of salt. (Make it look like the dipping bowls shitty trattorias bring to the table.) Slice each roll in half length-wise the way you would for a sandwich. Dunk each open faced piece into the oil and vinegar until surface is covered, adding more oil if needed.

2. Throw the bell peppers on the grill first (roasting by direct flame on the stove works) and cook until charred, rotating them every few minutes to cook evenly. Remove and sit them in a paper bag or a bowl with a lid (to help the skin peel off). After 10 minutes you'll rub the blackened skin off. Chop the peppers and set aside while you grill the bread.

3. Toss the dressed breads on your grill (a flat top or pan on the stove works in a pinch) and gently apply pressure with a spatula or your hands to grill evenly. Cook like this for a couple minutes, until grill marks develop. Turn the bread 45 degrees to get a cross-hatched grill mark. After another minute, flip the bread and grill the other side. Once bread is browned, on its way to charred, remove and set aside.

4. Prepare the rest of the salad: chop the stems off the caper berries and slice them in half. Slice the red onion in super-thin half moons. Wash and roughly chop the parsley; pick the smallest leaves of oregano and lemon basil for garnish.

5. Once bread has firmed up a bit but is still warm, chop into chunks and add everything to the bowl and dress with the tomato vinaigrette. Add salt or black pepper if desired and serve still warm.

Bro-tein

TO THE UNINITIATED, WE MUST APPEAR OBLIVIOUS TO THE FACT THAT the grill domain is primarily reserved for the flesh of beasts. Until this very literal instant, it might be possible to postulate that we two, perhaps, grew up in some kind of **cult where we worshiped donkeys, hugged tree trunks, and cried when one of the neighbors mowed their lawn. Nope.** We both grew up happily eating Happy Meals, shoving corndogs down our Hawaiian punch-stained gullets, and cramming Doritos and Lays into our face until our tongues were scratched and stinging.

We continue to chase those dreams, that innate junkie-esque jones to stop time and revert to Summer Feelings of corn syrup–spiked bliss. **Tiny diced onions, sad pickles, and one-note condiments coalescing on a sesame-seed bun—there's something right about that.** It haunted us, and we turned to laboratory experiments to simulate ground meat, and turned spice-heavy play-doh into clones of Dad's favorite dinner shortcut: Burgers 'n' stuff. **Drop these fake-outs down on your next cookout** and watch the kids jump out of your friends' skins.

HK Dogs Ⓥ

Makes 6

We don't care about Hebrew Nationals. Or Jimmy Dean. Or Dodger Dogs. The idea that any-one would miss eating pet food–grade meat shoved in a casing seems, frankly, insane. Now the feel of balancing a baby-soft seeded bun in one hand and that whiff of yellow mustard zig-zagging under your nose like a drunk driver's skid marks—that we've craved. Past summers, we've eschewed the bready veggie sausages and tofu pups from the store in favor of just eat-ing grilled vegetables. But making your own wieners from scratch is a whole 'nother ballgame. Fresh from the blender this witches' brew of spices, soy, beer, and flour smells so close to real we promise you'll have little kid summer camp flashbacks.

¼ cup plus 1 tablespoon
   raw almonds
9 ounces silken tofu
   (about a cup)
1 tablespoon Better Than
   Bouillon mushroom stock
⅔ cup water
3 tablespoons grapeseed oil
1 tablespoon onion powder
2 tablespoon smoked paprika
1 teaspoon sugar

1 teaspoon dried garlic
½ teaspoon liquid smoke
½ teaspoon mustard seeds
½ teaspoon mace (ground)
½ teaspoon cardamom (ground)
½ teaspoon coriander (ground)
1 cup wheat gluten
1 teaspoon arrowroot
wax paper
aluminum foil
canola spray

1. Throw the almonds in a (clean) coffee grinder and process them to dust. Throw this in your blender. Add every ingredient but the mushroom bouillon, water, arrowroot, and wheat gluten.

2. In a measuring cup, combine the bouillon and water to make broth, add arrowroot to this and whisk with a fork. Now pulse the entire mixture in the blender, slowly adding the broth, for about 1 minute. Stop and smell: it should smell like a processed hot dog. If it doesn't, you've done something wrong.

3. Dump this mixture into a large bowl and add the wheat gluten, stirring with a spatula until it becomes a unified mush with no flour clumps.

4. Fill a pot that contains a steam shelf with about 4 cups of water and set on high heat. Cover with a lid and ignore until you reach a boil.

5. Now you're ready to roll (your wieners): snip off eight pieces of wax paper with a length of about 4 inches, and lay them down in a row. Thoroughly spritz each one with canola spray. Now distribute eight equal portions of the mixture onto the parchment, trying your best to distribute the mix in a pile

that forms a line, not a ball. One at a time, roll each wiener package against the surface of your table or cutting board to force the mixture down toward the ends. Do what you gotta do to form a decent looking 6-inch sausage, making sure the thickness is con-sistent. Tipping the cylinder vertical, twist off the bottom end, like a New Year's party favor. The tighter you twist, the more round your hot dog's end will be. Flip and repeat with the other side. Repeat.

6. Now rip off aluminum foil strips about the size of your wax pieces and wrap each wiener in foil for extra shape support.

7. Gently lay the wieners down in the steam shelf of your boiling pot. (If you need to stack them, do so gently and evenly so they don't sit on a slant.) Cover with a lid.

8. Steam for 50 minutes, then remove from the steamer and let sit in their casings for about 20 minutes to firm up. Remove from their wax casing now so it doesn't stick to your wieners. Refrigerate until you wanna eat them.

9. To cook, grill over flames for just a couple minutes or sauté in a pan.

Beverage

Ballast Point,
Smoked Helles

Soundtrack

"Pussy Foot
the Duke,"
Comets on Fire

The "Maillard Fakeout" Burger Ⓥ

Makes 8 patties

The vegetarian hamburger is a constant conundrum. Most seekers oscillate between the bread-on-bread solution (seitan) and the "glue a mishmash of chopped veg into a hockey puck" maneuver (gardenburger ad infinitum). Ultimately, the goal is a facsimile of a thing that isn't really replicable without animal fat, connective tissue, and a little blood. Furrowed brows abound. Our experiments took a turn for the best when we focused on what makes burger eaters piss for joy—the umami explosion of a meat-based Maillard reaction (the browning of meat). We knew we couldn't get the exact texture of burnt muscle, but what if we could replicate the chemical reaction of seared flesh, which by all accounts is standard for a beefwich? Well, we did. And adding a few slices of roasted beet does nicely for that touch of hemoglobin we all so ravenously crave.

> 1 block extra firm tofu
> ½ cup olive oil
> ¼ cup soy sauce
> 1 portobello mushroom
> 10 shiitake mushrooms
> 1 white onion, minced
> 1 15-ounce can garbanzo beans
> 1 medium-sized white potato
> 1 red beet
> 1 teaspoon fresh black pepper
> 1 teaspoon sea salt

1. Press out as much moisture from your tofu as possible: slice the brick in half lengthwise, wrap it in towels, place a cutting board on top, and then dogpile as many pots on the board as feels safe. Let the crush do its thing for about 20 minutes.

2. At least 2 hours before you plan to cook the burgers, marinate the tofu: mush it up inside a Tupperware with a fork until you get a consistent, fine crumble. Add soy sauce and ¼ cup of the olive oil, top with a lid and let sit.

3. About 90 minutes later, prepare the rest of the burger fixins. Finely slice the shiitakes and the portobello. Place a cast-iron or large sauté pan on high heat and toss in the mushrooms bits. Toast like this for about 5 minutes, then add the minced onions and stir to combine. Now dump in the marinated tofu crumble, stir well to distribute the juices, and let cook on medium heat for 15 to 20 minutes, stirring a few times throughout, then remove from heat to cool.

4. Preheat your oven to 375 degrees. Take the whole beet and wrap it in aluminum foil.

5. Cut the potato into medium chunks, then put in a small sauce pot and cover with water. Cook on high heat until you reach a thorough boil, then remove from heat and let sit for another 5 minutes before removing. Shove the beet into the oven to roast for 30 minutes.

6. Strain the garbanzo beans, rinse, shake dry, and put them in a food processor. Pulse, adding the remaining olive oil to help it move. Toss in the potato chunks and pulse again until you have a mostly smooth bean-potato puree.

7. Combine the bean-potato puree with the cooked tofu-shrooms in a large bowl, mixing them together with your hands until you have one consistent mixture. Season with sea salt and black pepper. Let sit to marry.

Beverage

Odell, Double Pilsner

Soundtrack

"The Killing Moon," Echo and the Bunnymen

8. Remove your beet from the oven and let it rest for about 20 minutes, or until cool to handle. Once it is, gently rub off the peel (using the foil as a scrubber to keep your hands from being dyed red) and slice the beet into many thin slices using a mandoline.

9. Now you're ready to form your patties: pinch off a small handful (about ⅛ cup) of burger mixture and pat it between your hands like you're clapping, until you form a nice evenly round circle that's about 2 centimeters thick. Now grab a few slices of beet and slap this on top of your patty and rest this on your cutting board. Pinch off a

second handful of mixture and repeat to form a circle, and place this second patty on top of the first. Cupping it gently, press the two together and pat for 30 seconds or so until it forms one double patty with the beet slices cemented in the middle. Make sure the patty's surfaces are flat like a hockey puck and not oval. (Surface area for frying is good.)

10. Place the patties on a plate covered with wax paper and fridge 'em until you're ready to use. To cook, either pan fry for several minutes on each side until brown, or place a cast-iron on your outside grill to give you a flat outdoor cooking surface.

//////////

HEY YOU!

This recipe is even better if you char the peaches and tomatoes on the grill until they're skin blackens and they threaten to explode. The coal-induced sugar caramelization and smoke sting take this condiment to new Heitz.

//////////

Peach Ketchup Ⓥ

Makes 6 cups

Beverage

Alesmith, Yulesmith (Summer Release)

Soundtrack

"Summer Garden," Singapore Sling

2 pounds ripe peaches
1 pound ripe tomatoes
1 ¼ cups apple cider vinegar
¼ cup agave syrup
¼ cup brown sugar

¼ cup white sugar
1 tablespoon sea salt
6 bay leaves
6 whole cloves

1. Preheat your oven to 400 degrees. Pit and halve the peaches. Halve the tomatoes, and place both fruits face down on a baking sheet lined with parchment paper or with a light rubbing of oil. Shove in the oven to roast for about 20 minutes or until the skins are shriveling away from the fruit. (For bonus flavor, skip the oven and grill these suckers for 8 to 10 minutes or until lightly charred.)

2. Once removed from heat, let the fruit cool until easy to handle. Then remove their skins and toss the fruit in a blender or food processor. Pulse for a couple minutes until you have a consistent creamy texture.

3. Dump the puree in a large stock pot. Add sugars, vinegar, salt, and spices. Stir well and place on medium heat until you reach a bubbling boil. Reduce to simmer, cook this way for about an hour. Texture should reduce and thicken. Add more sugar to taste.

4. Strain the whole shebang, so you don't end up eating cloves and bay leaves.

Hot Tomato Water Ⓥ

Makes ¼ cup

2 orange tomatoes
2 habanero chiles, seeded and
 minced
1 ½ teaspoons white wine vinegar
½ teaspoon kudzu starch
sea salt and fresh black pepper
 to taste

1. Juice your tomatoes by cutting them in half and rubbing the cut side on the smallest holes of a box grater over a bowl. Rub till all you've got left is skin. Discard the skin and strain the resultant goo to create juice.

2. Stir in the vinegar and season with salt and pepper as you like. Then, and only then, add minced habanero. Place this in a sauce pot on medium-high heat, reserving 1 teaspoon of the tomato mixture. Combine reserved mixture in a small bowl with kudzu starch, stirring to dissolve. Let the mixture approach a boil.

3. Once you see the first signs of bubbles, add the starch and whisk every so often until you attain rolling boil. Let go another 30 seconds and remove from heat. Cool in a bowl. Sauce should thicken as it cools to hot sauce consistency. Be careful.

Beverage
Kern River, Just
Outstanding
IPA

Soundtrack
"Burger
Bar Baby,"
Alien Sex Fiend

Need a New Drug?
Kudzu Starch is it

These clumpy white powder rocks look more illicit than they actually are. Kudzu is a starch and a miracle thickener when used for gelling liquids. We got hooked after we added it to coconut milk on the stove and watched it seize up like a long-cooked custard. Now we toss it in anything that pours and watch it turn into something that jiggles. Tomato-water based hot sauce, for example. So what is this crack? It's a root and a vine that ancient basket-weaving dudes made the first Prada bags out of. It's also apparently a wonder drug that researchers think could be key to helping stop alcohol cravings in alcoholics...But if we can be considered legit test subjects, the white coats can pretty much rule out its effectiveness at that! Stick to using it in sauce, guys.

ⓥ Awesome Blossoms

Makes 20

Get over the preciousness of squash blossoms already; they are just nature's way of putting a pretty wrapper on gooey, fried gut-bombs. Don't be afraid to go nuts. Cheese and herbs is way too classic. What about slamming them with a carton of "animal-style" French fries, dripping with Thousand Island sauce and grilled onions? Cram all that shit in there. Even made vegan using wholesome summer produce, these awesome fritters belong next to fried Twinkies at the county fair.

Beverage

Deschutes,
Mirror Mirror

Soundtrack

"Triumph!!!,"
Shit Robot

HEY YOU!

Next level sand-wich? Put three of these monsters in a soft bun with some coleslaw and some sauce, and feel Oakland sandwich spot Bakesale Betty's ironclad hate-gaze.

"ANIMAL-STYLE" SAUCE
1 red onion, minced
1 white onion, minced
1 tablespoon grapeseed oil
⅔ cup veganaise
⅓ cup peach ketchup (pg. 57)
2 dill pickles, minced
sea salt to taste

20 squash blossoms
2 medium-sized potatoes
½ cup all-purpose flour
¼ cup cornmeal
½ teaspoon baking soda
¾ teaspoon salt
¾ plus ⅛ cup pale ale
2 cups canola oil (for frying)

1. To make animal-style sauce, sauté the finely minced onion in a pan with grapeseed oil over medium heat. Cook for at least 10 minutes, stirring often, until the onions start to turn nicely brown. Remove from heat and let cool for a couple minutes. In a mixing bowl combine the veganaise, ketchup, minced pickles, and sautéed onion. Add salt to taste. Set aside.

2. Cook the potatoes for your stuffing. Chop them roughly and add to a sauce pot with 2 cups of water. Place on high heat. When you hit a rolling boil, turn the heat off but let 'em continue to sit in the hot pot for 5 more minutes. Then drain.

3. Combine cooked potatoes and animal-style sauce in a bowl or pot that you can mash in, and take a potato masher to 'em until you get a creamy texture. (Doesn't have to be a puree, but shouldn't have massive chunks either.)

4. Gently stuff your blossoms, peeling one section of petal away enough to cram a tablespoon or so of your stuffing inside. Add a second tablespoon or so and then clasp your hands around the filled blossom, patting it together gently. Set on a plate and repeat until you have 20 stuffed blossoms. Stick these in the fridge for about an hour, or until ready to fry.

5. To fry, pour oil into a deep pot and place on high heat. While this gets hot, combine flour, baking soda, salt, and corn meal for a fry dredge. At the last minute, stir in the beer and whip with a fork until combined.

6. When oil's hot, batter and fry the blossoms a couple at a time. Dip one gingerly and turn it over to coat both sides; let some of the excess batter drip off but not all, then quickly but carefully drop in the pan. Fry for about 45 seconds on each side, or until almost dark brown, then flip with a spatula. Remove and let them sit on paper towels to drain. Repeat until they're all fried. Sprinkle each with salt and serve with extra ketchup.

Pickle Jar Potato Salad ⓥ

Serves 8 to 10

If you like pickles, you probably have an empty brine jar sitting in the door of your fridge right now. Or maybe a couple of them, sitting on ice like dead bodies you don't know how to dispose of...You can take the salt juice and all those spent herbs and spices that are left behind in a dill pickle jar and shake them awake into a lush dressing for potatoes. We like fingerlings, but it's equally good on new, red-skin potatoes. If your jar is mostly sad dill and a few peppercorns just bulk it up with some celery seeds and coriander seeds the night before.

PICKLE JAR DRESSING
2-3 small spring onions,
    bulb only
6 tablespoons jar pickle juice
4 tablespoons grain mustard
4 tablespoons grapeseed oil
1 tablespoon coriander seed

2 pounds small fingerling
    potatoes
½ cup celery leaves
1 tablespoon sesame seeds
1 tablespoon grapeseed oil
    (for sauté)

1. Start by making the dressing. Pour the pickle juice into a bowl through a fine mesh strainer to isolate the seeds, herbs, and any peppercorns that came with the jar. In a small sauté pan on low heat, toast these spices along with added coriander seeds for 2 to 3 minutes, shaking frequently to keep from browning. Once the coriander starts to pop, remove from heat.

2. Chop your spring onion bulbs (this should yield about a cup) and add to a small saucepan, cover with cool water and place on medium heat. Once you hit a boil, lower to a simmer and cook for another 5 to 8 minutes or until onion becomes soft and translucent. Strain the cooked onions and combine in a blender with pickle brine, mustard, and toasted spices. Pulse and slowly drizzle 3 tablespoons of the grapeseed oil. Taste dressing and either salt or add more brine as you like. Set dressing aside.

3. Slice the potatoes in half lengthwise and prepare to parboil, adding them to a pot of cool, salted water on high heat. While you wait for potatoes, pluck half a cup of celery leaves and wash them. As soon as you hit a legitimate boil, remove potatoes from the water and strain over the sink.

4. Finish them in a large sauté pan. Add remaining grapeseed oil and sauté for several minutes, adding sesame seeds for the last minute or so to toast. Potatoes are done once slightly browned and easy to bite.

5. Combine the dressing, celery, and cooked potatoes in a bowl. Add black pepper to taste. Serve warm if possible.

HEY YOU!

But guys, I only have jars of olives leftover in my fridge...Don't fret! Use the same proportions but sub blanched asparagus or green beans for the celery leaves. Then get some fucking pickles already!

Beverage

Rogue, Dad's
Little Helper
Black IPA

Soundtrack

"The Mad
Daddy,"
The Cramps

HEY YOU!

Vegetarian Curry Paste you ask? Yeah...90% of what's on the market has ground shrimp in it. Hunt down the 'yellow' and you should be gold. Mae Ploy is our preferred brand.

Beverage

The Bruery, Gunga Galunga

Soundtrack

"Babies," Pulp

Nasty Dates

Makes 20

You've stuffed a date before, right? Silky, explosive, sweet, and salty. Hot and kind of funky...Blue cheese–stuffed Medjools are nearly as rich as the now-ubiquitous bacon-wrapped dates, and thrown on a grill they're way better. They taste like rounding third base feels.

20 Medjool dates
8 ounces Mycella blue cheese
¼ cup red curry paste
10 wood skewers

1. Soak the skewers in water for about 10 minutes to prevent them from burning. Make sure your grill is hot.

2. While you wait, pit and stuff your dates: gently slit open each date and pry out the stone without causing structural damage to it. Using a butter knife, slather half a teaspoon or so of curry paste inside. Pinch off about a teaspoon of Mycella and wedge it inside too. Close the date back together.

(It should be gaping with cheese but stick together nicely.)

3. Once the skewers are sufficiently wet, shake them dry. Carefully insert each skewer through the center of one date and then a second. Spray the dates or the grill with a light layer of canola oil and lay them down to cook. Flip after 2 to 3 minutes. Once cheese starts to melt, they're ready to serve.

Junk Food Potato Salad

Serves 8 to 10

We'll never been the same after making blackened potato salad the first time. The idea is duh: parboil your cut potatoes, strain 'em and drain 'em, then shake 'em with cornmeal, herbs, and spices until they're coated and pan-fry them in fat to till they're crunchy. For our trademarked 'Dirty South' flavor, just use the Cajun crust from our okra gratin (pg. 71) which makes flavor crunchies out of fresh oregano, thyme, paprika, and white pepper. But for the 'Classic Americana' version, we do something we wouldn't normally do: we pop a bag of corn chips and use them lavishly like a fine imported spice. Whether it's a fancy schmancy brand or your guilty pleasure go-to Doritos, the technique is the same. Grind your chips into flavor-crystal crumbs using a food processor and dust those taters for blackening. Once you go blackened, you'll never go back.

2 pounds red skin potatoes
half a 17-ounce bag of corn chips
2 tablespoons butter
¼ cup mayonnaise
½ cup labneh or yogurt

½ cup scallions, sliced
½ cup fresh cilantro, chopped
sea salt to taste

1. Parboil the potatoes: dice them into cubes on the larger end of bite-sized. Add them to a pot of salted water. Set on medium and cook until you reach a rolling boil. Remove and strain the potatoes immediately, letting them cool in a colander for a couple minutes.

2. Dump half a bag of your preferred corn chips into your food processor in a couple batches, depending on size of the processor, and blend for 20 seconds or so to create fine chip crumbs (should yield at least 2 cups). Set aside.

3. Combine mayonnaise, yogurt, scallions, and chopped herbs and set aside.

4. Heat a large skillet or cast-iron on high heat and once it's hot, turn to medium and add butter. Add the potatoes and sauté for 3 minutes. (Taste a potato, it should be cooked, but pert, not soft or crumbly.) When you're happy with them, add the chip crumbs and gently toss to coat. (Some of the crumbs will stick to the potatoes, some will bounce around the pan, this is fine.) Cook for another 2 minutes to lightly toast the crumbs, then remove from heat.

5. In a large bowl, gently mix the potatoes with the dressing. Garnish with extra chip crumbs, taste, and salt to your liking.

Beverage

Oskar Blues, Mama's Little Yella Pils

Soundtrack

"Suicide Sally and Jonny Guitar," Primal Scream

BBQ Mosh Pit

A WHILE BACK, A BROOKLYN COUPLE EMAILED US ASKING IF WE WOULD CATER THEIR JULY WEDDING: A VEGETARIAN SOUTHERN BARBECUE. Cooking outside in tents. For 100 friends and family. From **rural Kentucky**. Who loved their pork. Yup.

This could be the beginning of an ugly catering war story, but it's not. After we boned up on our **okra, cornbread, and black-eyed pea recipes**, we settled on a massive bourbon-friendly feast that kept even their backwoods uncle happy. Along the way we gleaned that southern cooking is just good cooking, best done outdoors with plenty of sun-warmed fruits and herbs, buckets of red vinegar, cornmeal crusts satisfyingly blackened, and **sweet, slow-simmered sauces** puckery enough to cut through butter or grease.

Years after Eli and Tamara's wedding, we still reach for these recipes for fried po' boys, hearty stews, and tangy slaws for all manner of **summer parties and patio cookouts,** or really whenever we feel the urge to wade into the BBQ (mosh) pit and start **crushing skulls**.

Oyster Po' Boys

Makes 6

Best vegan sandwich, ever. (Notice the period.) We fill our po' boys, those traditionally vulgar-sized submarine sandwiches spilling over with fried crustaceans or bivalves, with thrice-cooked oyster mushrooms. The cumulative effect is dirty beyond words. Fluffy bread, cool cabbage shreds, and steaming, crisp-on-the-outside, juicy-on-the-inside mushroom fritters, slathered with slightly funky radish cream and a line of vinegary hot sauce to keep things interesting. The times we've served these for wads of cash on the back patio of our favorite bars, drunkards go ga-ga. Most tweeted sandwich award.

FRIED "OYSTERS"
½ pound oyster mushrooms
1 ½ tablespoons olive oil
sea salt to taste
½ cup all-purpose flour
¼ cup cornmeal
½ teaspoon baking powder
½ teaspoon sea salt, plus more
  to taste
¾ cup pale ale,
  plus 1 tablespoon

2 ½ cups grapeseed or canola
  oil for frying

6 soft hoagie buns
½ cup shredded green cabbage
¼ cup radish remoulade (pg. 11)
3 teaspoons Louisiana hot sauce

1. Prepare mushrooms by tearing each into strips (in half if small, into quarters if big). Put a sauté pan on high heat, add olive oil, and toss in mushroom strips. Cook for 2 to 3 minutes, shaking or stirring often, or until shrooms begin to release their liquid and some pieces start to brown. Remove and set aside to cool. (To double or triple recipe, roast shrooms for 6 minutes on a tray in a 350-degree oven instead of on stove.)

2. Set a deep pot filled with the frying oil over a high flame. Let heat 8 to 10 minutes. Meanwhile, prepare a fry batter by mixing the flour, cornmeal, salt, and baking powder. Then add the beer slowly and whisk with a fork until creamy and wet enough to coat mushrooms. (Add tablespoon more beer if it seems too dry.)

3. Batter a test shroom. Dip a mushroom strip into fry batter, shake off excess, and carefully drop into hot oil. It should immediately sizzle and brown within 30 seconds. Your oil is hot.

4. Repeat with a small handful of shrooms at a time, coating them and smooshing them loosely together to form a garbled ball. Drop in the oil and flip after 15 to 20 seconds using tongs, slotted spoon, or a spider. Once golden, but not brown, fish them out, and let drip dry on paper towels.

5. Wait for the shrooms to cool and relax and then drop them again for another 5 seconds to make crisp. Remove.

6. Serve by opening each bun and pinching out about a teaspoon of extra bread to make room for your sprinkling of cabbage topped by the oysters. Slather bread with remoulade, place shrooms and cabbage, then finish with a line of hot sauce.

HEY YOU!

Do you really need to sauté AND fry these fuckers twice? Oh yes you do. But if you got people coming over, you can do everything but the last fry and do 'em to order lightening fast.

Beverage
Brewdog, Tokyo

Soundtrack
"Rebel, Rebel,"
David Bowie

Summer Sauce Ⓥ

Makes 2 liters

We badly wish that drowning fries, pizza, and burgers in barbecue sauce wasn't so dang nasty. But your store-bought "masterpiece" is just corn syrup, Heinz paste, and reconstituted onion powder dyed the color of tar. Replace that obesity wonder-tonic with the real shit: roasted tomatoes and caramelized onions kicked up with good vinegar and made tangy with peaches. There are two ways we make this summer sauce depending on what it's smothering. The real good shit comes from smoking about 2 pounds of jackfruit over hickory chips (follow directions for jackfruit carnitas on page 13), combine with the sauce base and serve. If the sauce is gonna top anything else (fries, pizza, or burgers, duh) we get wood-smoke taste by adding 2 teaspoons of smoked salt, or a single teaspoon of liquid smoke.

Beverage

Craftsman, Fireworks Saison

Soundtrack

"Summer Song," YACHT

//////////

HEY YOU!

Just sauce? Hell no, this is an entire meal if combined with the smoked jackfruit we taught you about earlier. Sub this BBQ sauce into the recipe on page 13 to rule the backyard.

//////////

VINEGAR BASE
½ cup water
2 tablespoons brown sugar
1 ½ cups apple cider vinegar
1 ½ tablespoons smoked
    paprika
2 teaspoons salt
2 teaspoons black pepper

2 white onions
4 tablespoons margarine
    or butter

6 cloves garlic
2 teaspoons cumin seed
2 teaspoons caraway seed
2 cups Peach Ketchup
    (pg. 57)
2 cups vinegar base (above)
2 teaspoons Dijon mustard
4 tablespoons molasses
2 tablespoons maple syrup
sea salt to taste

1. Make the vinegar base. Combine water with vinegar in a saucepan on high heat, and once hot stir in brown sugar to dissolve. Add smoked paprika, salt, and pepper, and remove to cool.

2. Measure out all your wet ingredients, except the margarine, and whisk together in a measuring cup, including the vinegar base. Set aside.

3. Mince the onions. Put a large sauce pot on medium heat, add the margarine. Add onion,

cooking until translucent but not caramelized, about 3 minutes.

4. Add the garlic, cumin, and caraway to the onions to toast for 3 minutes.

5. Now, pour in wet ingredients and give a hefty stir. Let cook on low for 20 to 30 minutes, stirring every few. The goo should be sputtering. Remove and let cool. Puree in a blender until smooth and all onion chunks are gone. Serve cold or warm.

Kaleslaw (V)

Serves 15

Sitting limp and milky in a plastic shooter like semen in a used condom, coleslaw is the stuff of crappy diners. Like bad sex, you wish you hadn't asked for it. Kaleslaw by contrast is the side-dish stud of any backyard barbecue for two simple reasons: all women love kale, and the stiffy green cannot be tamed with even the staunchest lipid-dressing, let alone go limp in a cup. This salad goes all night.

4 heads of Russian kale
6 large carrots
half a white onion
half a red cabbage
2 lemons (zested)

SLAW DRESSING
2 ½ cups veganaise
1 tablespoon Dijon mustard
1 teaspoon Louisiana hot sauce
zest of 2 lemons
8–10 lemon verbena leaves
 (optional)
2 teaspoons fresh black pepper
2 teaspoons kosher salt

1. Prepare the kale for its rubdown: take each leaf and cut off the bottom few inches of stem, then carefully remove as much of the rib as possible by slicing a "V" into the leaf, without actually disassembling the leaf (you want whole, flat surfaces to chop into even, long pieces).

2. Rinse and cut kale: on a cutting board, slice each large leaf like you might chiffonade basil.

3. Zest both your lemons into a large mixing bowl, making sure to get every last inch of yellow goodness. Save zest for the dressing. Then slice and juice lemons into a separate container. In a large bowl, cover kale with filtered water and add the fresh lemon juice (do this in two phases if needed).

4. Take one small bunch of soaking leaves at a time and massage the kale by scrunching as hard as you can. Repeat for several minutes. Let soak in the lemon-water for at least 30 minutes, covered in the fridge (or as long as overnight).

5. After kale has sat as long as you want, remove it from fridge and drain, then work in a salad spinner until completely dry.

6. Grate the carrot on a cheese grater, shred cabbage super-thin using a mandoline.

7. Make slaw dressing. Combine veganaise with black pepper, salt, lemon zest, mustard, and hot sauce. Add minced lemon verbena if using. Whisk to make dressing (it should be thick and creamy, not thin).

8. Combine carrot and kale and toss with dressing and let sit in fridge until ready to eat. Add the cabbage right before serving so as not to turn the whole thing purple.

Beverage

Lagunitas, Little
Sumpin' Wild

Soundtrack

"Raw Ramp,"
T. Rex

Blackened Okra Gratin

Serves 8

This is a study in textural brain-bombing: a crunch, ooze, slurp, goo game that will plant your ass face-first in a blissed-out mess. Okra, typically relegated to overcooked stews, either frightens or fascinates eaters with its ever building slime levels. This one's for the Okra Geek who loves goo, but also the Okra Pansy who can't get over its similarity to certain bodily excretions. Our Mornay sauce (to end all Mornay sauce) both hides and elevates the creamy, slimy explosion. It's a dish meant for attacking in gangs, the way Mardi Gras drunkards hover over a table of spice-rubbed crawfish and pry at them with wild abandon, or the damned cower in Hieronymous Bosch paintings. It's extravagant and deliciously repulsive, but why would you want it any other way?

MORNAY SAUCE
2 tablespoons butter
1 shallot, skinned and halved
7 whole cloves
⅛ cup all-purpose flour
1 ½ cups organic whole milk
4 ounces Landaff, grated
4 ounces Gruyère, grated
4 ounces Parmagiano Reggiano, grated
¼ teaspoon ground white pepper
sea salt to taste

VEG
2 pounds fresh okra
1 pound Korean green peppers, Padrons or Shishitos
2 tablespoons extra virgin olive oil
1 teaspoon sea salt (preferably sel gris de Guerande)

CAJUN CRUST
⅛ cup cornmeal
1 teaspoon smoked paprika
½ tablespoon fresh thyme, chopped
½ tablespoon fresh oregano, chopped
½ teaspoon ground white pepper
½ teaspoon black pepper

Beverage

Russian River, Pliny the Elder

Soundtrack

"Ain't It a Shame," Nirvana

1. Stab the halved shallot's exposed face full of cloves and then cover with the milk in a small saucepan. Heat on medium about 10 minutes, but don't let it boil.

2. Make the Mornay: melt the butter in a medium saucepan on medium heat. When it starts to foam add half the flour and combine with a whisk. After its incorporated, add the second half and combine. (At this point the roux will be the texture of wet cookie dough.) Keep cooking. The doughy jam will melt a little, until the roux foams and starts to turn toasty brown.

3. When brown, add ¼ cup of the warm milk and whisk until it looks like a dough is forming. Repeat until you've got what looks like a thick paste. Then continue adding the milk until its gone (don't add the shallot). When all the milk is mixed in and you've got a lady's-undies-smooth-sauce turn the heat to low and trade your whisk for a spatula.

4. Divide all three cheeses in half. Pick one and add half in small handfuls to the pan. (Fight the urge to shove the rest in your mouth.) Whisk until the cheese is melted and repeat with next two cheeses (reserving half of each for later). Season with white pepper and salt. Taste it. Fucked up good? Set it aside while you toast the okra.

5. Heat a cast-iron skillet until she's smoking. Cut the okra into ½-inch rounds and toss 'em in the pan dry. Cook about 10 minutes, shaking every so often until their faces are charred a little. On another stovetop, toast the peppers over an open flame about 5 minutes, rotating until they blister. Toss them in a paper bag to cool for 5 minutes. Then rub off as much blistered skin as you can. Chop into pieces equal in size to the okra.

6. Preheat your oven to 400 degrees. In a mixing bowl, toss the toasted okra and peppers with olive oil and sea salt. Add the remaining half of the grated Landaff and Gruyère and ¾ of the sauce and mix.

7. In a 10 x 10-inch casserole dish, ladle the extra Mornay sauce to cover the bottom. Add the amazing mess in your mixing bowl on top and distribute evenly.

8. Lastly, make your crust by combining the leftover grated Parm with the spices, herbs, and cornmeal. Sprinkle this over the gooey cheesy veggie mess until you can't see any white. Bake in the oven for 10 to 15 minutes. Check if middle is melting. Once it is, crank oven to broil. Broil for 2 to 4 minutes, just until the crust is blackened and crazy smelling. Serve.

///////////

HEY YOU!

What is Landaff and why does it rule? It's a ripping raw cow's milk tomme from New Hampshire and it'll make your gratin into silk.

///////////

Succotash "Stew" Ⓥ

Serves 6

Eating soup in the summer sounds like chugging Gatorade Ice in a blizzard. This is not that. This is like a warm drizzle after sunset or something to make you sweat just enough to notice a breeze. Be thankful it blew you. This is a vegetable medley that cooks for seconds in your bowl. Oh yeah, it still takes a minimum of 4 hours to make. Good things and waiting? Yeah. It's true.

Beverage

North Coast, Prankster

Soundtrack

"Draw Your Breaks," Scotty

BEANS & BROTH
2 cups marrow beans
3 quarts water
2 tablespoons salt
4 sprigs of cilantro
4 sprigs of parsley
4 sprigs of thyme
1 sprig of rosemary
10 chives
2 cups witbier (like Prankster)

FRESH GARNISH
6 shiso leaves
1 red onion
3 ripe tomatoes (diced
    ¼-inch thick)
¼ cup picked cilantro leaves
1 ripe avocado, diced
6 teaspoons of olive oil
1 teaspoon of white wine
    vinegar
black pepper

1. In a large stock pot combine the beans, the water, and the salt. Heat on medium until bubbles start to burble. Reduce to low. Clump the thyme, cilantro, rosemary, parsley on top of each other and then tie 'em all up with the chives. Plant this herb seedbomb in under the bobbling beans, cover the pot, and simmer on low for 3 hours.

2. Test the beans. They should be cooked through with only just a hint of snap to them. Strain them from their broth, pass the broth through a strainer, and discard the herbs. You can keep the beans covered with broth in the fridge covered for 3 days.

3. To prepare the rest of the "stew," heat the strained broth with the witbier. Taste it for salt and add to your liking.

4. Skin the onion and cut in half lengthwise, then slice on a mandoline for thin half moons. Place the slices in a bowl and cover with cool water and a splash of champagne vinegar and move on.

Nice Buns
how to pimp your hoagie

The secret to the best Po' Boy may be what's outside, not inside. Most southern barbecue joints fail at this, using big-ass French rolls made outta corn syrup and skull-white bleached flour. Tastes like nothing and it's cheap. We get it, but why settle when you can find ones that taste like bread should taste and are still cheap. Our ah-ha moment was finding a Mexican bakery down the street that pumps out fresh bolillos several times a day. They're perfect oval rolls all dusty and crusty outside, warm and soft-as-a-sponge inside. They smell like yeast. We had a scare at first when one of the ladies told us they were made with lard. Vegetable-lard as it turned out. A little fat never hurt no one! These make ideal vehicles for fried fritters as well as tender, saucey gobs of smoked fillings. No Mexican bakery down the street? Open one.

5. In separate bowls, assemble thusly: one shiso leaf on bottom, about ½ cup strained beans, a few sprigs of onions and cilantro, diced tomato, and a dice of avocado. Top each assembled bowl with two twists from your pepper mill and a teaspoon of olive oil.

6. Once broth has attained a boil, top each bowl with ½ cup of the scalding liquid. Alert your diners to wait 4 minutes for the soup to "steep," then watch them maul.

Cool Ranch Biscuits

Makes about 10 biscuits

Pushing snack aisle flavors like "Vivaldi Onion Fondue" or "Thai Expressions" or "Hawaiian Teriyaki Pizza Skewers" seems so common-place now, but "Cool Ranch" is the OG. We've sprinkled our ranchy blend of herbs and spices on almost everything and decided biscuits are the snack aisle flavor show stealers. Short of trying these as donuts, these couldn't be more addictive...Hmm, donuts...

2 cups all-purpose flour, plus extra for kneading
1 stick of butter (½ cup)
1 ½ teaspoons baking powder
½ teaspoon baking soda
¾ teaspoon kosher salt
1 cup cool ranch dressing (pg. 94)

Beverage
Victory,
Prima Pils

Soundtrack
"Range Life,"
Pavement

1. Crank your oven to 500 degrees.

2. Grab your butter from the fridge, slice it up into a handful of tablespoon-sized pads, and stick them on a plate and back in the fridge. (Cold butter is key.)

3. Make your cool ranch dressing, or remove it from the fridge. Prep a lightly greased baking sheet and get out a rolling pin and a biscuit cutter, preferably about 2 inches in diameter (use any deep lid as a cutter in a pinch).

4. Measure and combine the flour, baking powder, baking soda, and salt in a large bowl, mixing well. Then remove the cold butter and add it to the bowl. Using your hands, squish the butter together with the dry ingredients, working quickly, until you have a crumb-like consistency. (Do not over-mix, this will melt the butter.)

5. Pour about ¾ cup of the cool ranch into the bowl and mix with a spoon or your hands until the mixture comes together into a slightly tacky ball. If it remains too dry to bring together, add more ranch, one tablespoon at a time, until you can gather it together.

6. Dust a cutting board with flour and knead the dough for 30 seconds to 1 minute, adding more flour as needed, until you have a uniform ball that doesn't stick to the board or your hands. Using the rolling pin, flatten the ball until it's about a half-inch thick. Cut 10 to 12 biscuits and place them on the baking sheet so that they gently touch one another.

7. Shove in the oven for eight to 10 minutes. They should rise to nearly double their original size. Once browned slightly, remove and let sit about 5 minutes. Serve with butter and sea salt.

Kill Your Idols (V) Cornbread

Serves 2 dozen

Ugh, god, boring. Looking up a cornbread recipe feels like googling "how to tie your shoes." It's so brain dead they print it on the box of cornmeal. But that's okay, because we're about to make you feel special by teaching tricks that no box knows: you start this bread the day before, soaking it in a vegan fake-out concoction for buttermilk. Add flax meal instead of egg, replace the honey with brown rice syrup, fold fresh corn into the batter, and coat the entire thing with jalapeño glaze. Fuck off Betty Crocker.

SOAKER
4 cups almond milk
2 teaspoons cider vinegar
2 cups cornmeal

BREAD
6 tablespoons flax meal
1 ⅛ cups water
4 cups all-purpose flour
3 teaspoons baking powder
¾ teaspoons baking soda
1 cup brown sugar
1 cup white sugar
3 teaspoons sea salt
6 tablespoons margarine, plus 2 for glaze
4 tablespoons brown rice syrup, plus 2 for glaze
2 jalapeños, minced
3 cups fresh corn (off the cob)

Beverage

New Belgian, Clutch

Soundtrack

"Bionic Rats," Lee Scratch Perry

///////////

HEY YOU!

For a deeper loaf you can bake this in your cast-iron skillet, but since big groups maul for this stuff we prefer square portions. Serve this with succotash stew.

///////////

1. The night before you bake, mix the almond milk and vinegar in a large bowl, and add the cornmeal. Cover with plastic wrap and let sit on the counter overnight.

/////////// **The Next Day** ///////////

2. Preheat the oven to 350 degrees. Prepare the dry ingredients and wet ingredients separately. In a small bowl, combine flax and water and let sit for 5 minutes. In a large bowl, sift the flour, baking powder, baking soda, and salt.

3. Put the margarine in a small saucepan on medium heat until melted (or in a bowl in the microwave for 20 seconds) and add the brown rice syrup. Remove from heat and add this to the flax water mixture. Add sugars and whisk. Fold this mixture into the soaked cornmeal and mix well.

4. Now stir in the dry ingredients, mixing well until there are no clumps and no dry bits clinging to the bowl. Finally, add fresh corn and stir just until distributed.

5. Pour this batter onto a well-greased 8 x 11-inch baking sheet. The batter should come up to each side but not threaten to spill over. Place the pan in the oven and cook for 30 minutes.

6. On the stove, melt additional margarine with additional brown rice syrup and and minced jalapeño to make the glaze.

7. Check the cornbread after 30 minutes. Stick in a knife or toothpick; it should come out clean. Brush the top of the bread with the jalapeño glaze and shove back in the oven for another 5 to 8 minutes or until the sides start to brown slightly. Remove and let cool for 20 minutes before cutting.

Potlatches

WHEN IT COMES TO THE POTLUCK, WE PREFER TO RECOGNIZE ITS origins in the traditions of the Kwakwaka'wakw people of the Pacific Northwest. (Uh hum. Don't know where we're going with this one, do you...) A central tenet of their cultural philosophy was that **wealth meant sharing commodities, rather than hording them.** The "potlatch," a gathering focused on feasting, shimmying, and gift-giving, was made "next level shit" by the **Kwakwaka'wakw**—after all this loot was exchanged, it was destroyed. (Partly due to all the poisoned and diseased crap white traders used as chemical warfare, but forget that for a second.) Today, the potluck follows this same pattern: collective toil (cooking), for collective gift-giving (the presenting of crock pots, casseroles, and Tupperware), group destruction of property (ravenous eating, seconds and thirds) **then finally, collective nurture and growth from all this raging.**

Do we really consider a potluck to be an **anarcho-syndicalist assassination of the self,** like some outdoor cannibalistic self-decapitation-of-the-singular-spirit? Well, yeah, sure. But, like, less...brutal. Bring a little bit of collectivity with you to your next group outing and rekindle the flames of the many. **Eat your riches, and your friends—their riches! Not them!**

Mezze Mecca

This is our Arab Spring. If badasses in Iran, Syria, and Egypt can learn to use Twitter to take over the streets, hopefully we Americans can at least learn a few tricks from the Middle East on how to make radical picnic food that doesn't require cutlery. We take our picnics sitting down, cross-legged on blankets, leaving no place for forks and knives. In our version of heaven, there are 70 untouched dips and spreads—oil-slicked but still velvety enough to make the magic carpet ride from hand to mouth on nothing but a hunk of homemade bread. Whether you stone-bake soft pita or grill a hearty garbanzo flatbread over fire, if you eat this way, you no longer need a fork, spoon, or knife. And forget plates. Get down on your knees and prey.

Artichoke Hummus ⓥ

Serves 10 to 12

ARTICHOKE BRAISE
2 whole artichokes
1 cup pitted Manzanilla olives
1 cup Manzanilla olive brine
1 cup filtered water
2 teaspoons champagne vinegar
3 tablespoons olive oil
1 teaspoon sea salt
1 lemon

HUMMUS
1 ½ cups dried garbanzo beans
   (or 3 cups cooked, about 2
   15-ounce cans)
⅛ cup fresh lemon juice
¼ cup tahini
½ cup plus 2 tablespoons
   olive oil
4 cloves garlic, peeled
sea salt to taste

Beverage

Lost Abbey,
Red Barn Ale

Soundtrack

"This Must be
the Place,"
Talking Heads

HEY YOU!

Are cooked dry beans better for this recipe than canned ones? Was Erasmus all about free will? Duh!

1. First, prep the artichokes. (This can be done only 2 hours before making hummus, but is even better the night before.) Remove the first, lowest layer of leaves and discard. Slice both chokes in half vertically, from their tip to their base. Using a paring knife and a spoon, cut out the prickly center and spoon out the fine thistles, and discard them.

2. Strain your olives over a bowl to get a cup of olives and a cup of brine. Mix your braising liquid by combining the olive brine, water, vinegar, olive oil, and salt. Cut the lemon in half and squeeze the juice into your braising mix. Reserve the squeezed halves for the braise. Roughly chop the olives.

3. Place the 4 artichoke halves face down in a large, thick-bottomed pot. Add the braising liquid (it wont cover the chokes), your squeezed out lemon halves, and the chopped olives. Place this on the stove over medium heat. Once it hits a boil, lower to simmer and cook covered for about 45 minutes. Watch to make sure liquid doesn't cook off completely. Turn off heat and let sit covered for another 30 minutes, plus a final 30 minutes uncovered to cool. (Skip the next step if you're making right away.)

4. Put the artichoke halves into a large food-grade, zippable plastic bag and cover with the brine and olives. Push out as much air as possible and close. Stick in the fridge overnight. If cooking garbanzo beans, soak them in 4 cups water.

/////////// **The Next Day** ///////////

5. Cook soaked beans now: strain and add to a pot with 4 cups fresh water and cook on high heat until you reach a boil, then lower to simmer for about an hour or until fully cooked. Strain and cool to use.

6. Remove the artichokes from their flavor bag. Skin the outer layer of rough peel off the stem. Now make a cut at the base of the leaves to separate the artichoke heart. (Reserve the leaves and brine.) Place chopped artichoke hearts in your food processor. Combine the garbanzo beans, tahini, and lemon in the processor and pulse. Slowly drizzle the olive oil, save for the last 2 tablespoons.

7. Measure out ⅔ cup of brine. Keep pulsing and add to blender. Keep blending and add remaining brine as desired, tasting along the way.

8. Top with extra olive oil and a sprinkling of the leftover braised olives. Serve with the braised artichoke leaves.

Campfire Caviar Ⓥ

Serves 10 to 12

3 medium-sized eggplants
1 head garlic
½ cup tahini
½ cup plus 1 tablespoon lemon juice
¼ cup olive oil
¾ cup curly parsley, chopped
1 tablespoon sea salt

HEY YOU!

Any of the drippings from these roasted eggplants should go straight in the mix, it's liquid smoke. You could bottle it.

Beverage

Great Divide, Belgian Imperial Stout

Soundtrack

"On Green Dolphin Street," Lionel Hampton

1. Prepare the eggplants. First poke each one several times with a fork; do it evenly. You'll be roasting a head of garlic with them, so wrap the garlic in foil with a drizzle of olive oil.

2. Now, cook the eggplants to smithereens. Preheat the oven to 375 degrees, then set each eggplant on a stovetop burner for several minutes. Rotate using tongs once the skin blackens. Once blackened, lay them in a large ceramic roasting pan and slide into the oven for about 10 to 12 minutes to fully cook, adding the foil-wrapped garlic. Once done, let the charred eggplants sit for at least 15 minutes to cool.

3. While you wait for eggplants to cool, measure out the tahini, oil, and lemon juice in a mixing bowl. Wash and pat dry the parsley, finely chop it, and add that too.

4. Once the eggplants are cool enough to handle, gently peel off and discard their charred skin. Do it one at a time over a colander inside another large bowl, making sure not to waste the flesh. Let the flesh sit in the colander to drain for a few minutes, catching any excess of the brown eggplant juices in the bowl. Add to this any juice that's pooled in the roasting dish. Chop up the flesh and add to your bowl of ingredients. Add the roasted garlic and give this mixture a thorough mashing with a large fork.

5. Mix together all ingredients and salt to taste. Now, add the cooked eggplant juice to taste. It gives you that perfect campfire-smoke flavor.

Falafel Salad Ⓥ

Serves 8 to 10

1 cup dry garbanzo beans
1 pound fresh fava beans
1 cup coarse bulgur wheat
4 tablespoons olive oil, divided in half
2 packed cups parsley leaves
1 tablespoon cumin seed

2 teaspoons coriander seed
1 cup yogurt
2 cloves garlic
1 lemon, juiced
sea salt and cracked black pepper to taste

Beverage

North Coast, Le Merle Saison

Soundtrack

"Merciful Sword," Cuticle

1. The night before serving, soak the garbanzo beans in 4 cups of water.

/////////// **The Next Day** ///////////

2. Strain and rinse the garbanzo beans, then add them to a medium-sized pot and cover with 3 to 4 cups of water and bring to a boil. Reduce heat to a simmer and cook covered for about 1 hour.

3. Bring a large pot of salted water to a boil while you prepare the fava beans. Rip the beans from their comfy home and wait for the water to boil. Set up an ice bath next to your pot for shocking the beans. When the water is boiling, add the favas in batches of 1 cup at a time. They are done when they all float to the top; scoop them out with a strainer and toss them in the ice bath until cold. When they are cool enough to handle, slip them out of their skins by pinching open the top of each bean with your fingernail, give a squeeze and the beans will pop right out.

4. Bring 2¼ cups of salted water to boil in yet another pot, and add the bulgur. Boil the grains for 5 minutes, then lower the heat and simmer for an additional 20 minutes. Strain off excess water.

5. Set your oven to 400 degrees. Combine the two types of beans on one sheet pan, and dump the bulgur on another. Toss both with 2 tablespoons olive oil each and spread evenly across each pan. Throw both pans in the oven and bake for 30 minutes, removing them after every 10 minutes to agitate. The beans should start to brown slightly and the bulgur should be crispy.

6. Toast the cumin and coriander in a small sauté pan on medium heat until they start to pop. Grind them in a mortar and pestle or a clean coffee grinder.

7. In a mortar and pestle, smash the two cloves of garlic with a pinch of salt to make a paste. Add 1 tablespoon of yogurt, mix, and then add the yogurt garlic paste to the remaining yogurt. Add the lemon juice and the toasted, ground spices. Taste and adjust the seasoning.

8. To serve, give the parsley leaves a rough chop and combine with the toasted beans and bulgur. Dress with the yogurt sauce, or leave it on the side.

Beverage

Jolly Pumpkin,
Bam Noir

Soundtrack

"Mehmet
Emmi," Selda

Malted Muhamarra Ⓥ

Serves 10 to 12

8 bell peppers
3 cups walnuts
1 cup breadcrumbs
¼ cup grapeseed oil
2 tablespoons smoked paprika
½ teaspoon cayenne pepper
2 tablespoons malt barley syrup
1 ½ tablespoons sea salt

1. Char the peppers by throwing them on the grill for 4 to 5 minutes, or, if cooking inside, char them on the stovetop by sitting two peppers on each stovetop burner. Rotate the peppers using tongs once the skin blackens. Repeat until all the peppers are completely black.

2. Sit the charred peppers in a paper bag or a Tupperware container with a lid. Let them cool like this for 10 to 20 minutes so the skins will loosen. Then take one at a time and rub the blackened skin off, being careful not to burst the peppers and lose their juice. Gently remove the core and the seeds and discard. Once all the peppers are rubbed clean, cut each into three or four large pieces and set aside.

3. Toast the walnuts (reserving half for later use) on very low heat, shaking often to keep them from burning. This should take about 10 minutes. Remove from heat.

4. In a food processor, combine walnuts, peppers, and all other ingredients except for the reserved half cup of nuts and the bread-crumbs. Pulse, stopping to taste, and salt as you like. Dump your beautiful red mixture into a mixing bowl and add breadcrumbs. Chop remaining walnuts finely and add those too. Let sit for at least an hour before serving.

Pink Pita Ⓥ

Makes about 15

3 raw medium-sized beets
½ cup water
3 cups bread flour, plus extra
    for dusting

2 teaspoons sea salt
2 teaspoons yeast
2 tablespoons olive oil
1-2 tablespoons za'atar

1. Two hours before baking, prepare the dough. Peel the beets and place in a blender with the water. Pulse for more than a minute until thoroughly pulverized into a red beet juice. Over a bowl, push the juice through fine mesh strainer using a ladle. You should have about 1 ¼ cups liquid; if you don't, add water till you do. Add salt and olive oil to this and whisk.

2. In a large mixing bowl, combine the flour and yeast and mix. Now, pour the beet juice mixture into the bowl and mix with your hands until it comes together to form a slightly sticky ball.

3. Transfer the dough to a floured cutting board. Flour your mitts, then knead the dough for 5 minutes and cover with a towel and rest it for 5 minutes. Come back, apply more flour to the surface and knead again for about 8 minutes or until the dough becomes silky smooth.

4. Let the dough rise. Place it in a large mixing bowl that's been drizzled with olive oil. Cover the bowl with plastic wrap and sit it on the counter for at least 90 minutes, until it doubles in size.

5. Return the risen dough to a floured surface, and cut it into 12 equal-sized pieces. Roll these into balls and gently press each into flat circles using a tortilla press, making sure to spray the press with canola oil to keep from sticking. (A rolling pin works fine too.) Lay the pita discs flat on a baking sheet, cover with a towel and let sit for 10 minutes. They'll shrink a little. (If baking, preheat oven to 475 degrees with a pizza stone or cast-iron inside. If grilling, start your grill.)

6. After 10 minutes, repeat. Press more firmly than last time in order to help the pita discs keep their stretched-out shape. Lay them back on the baking sheet and sprinkle each with za'atar. Cover and let sit another 8 minutes. Spray, or lightly mist, with water and let sit another 2 minutes before cooking.

7. Take pita one or two at a time and place on the pizza stone, cast-iron, or straight onto the lightly greased grill. Cook for about 3 minutes or until the top bubbles and the bottom side browns slightly. Remove and let cool.

Beverage

Left Hand,
Milk Stout

Soundtrack

"Fire," Valet

HEY YOU!

Degas your dough! Punch down your inflated balls before you shape them so they'll rise a little bit more prior to baking. This'll help you get those air pockets in your pita, and keep the flatbreads fluffy.

Garbanzo Flatbreads

Makes 6

2 ⅓ cups all-purpose flour
1 cup garbanzo bean flour
2 teaspoons sea salt
1 teaspoon instant yeast
2 tablespoons olive oil, plus 2 teaspoons divided
2 tablespoons honey
1 cup water

1. Combine the flours, yeast, and salt in a mixing bowl and blend with the olive oil, water, and honey. Mix together until everything forms into a ball—use the ball to scrape the sides of the bowl until every last bit of flour is attached to the beany amoeba.

2. Knead the dough on a well-floured surface for 10 to 15 minutes. The dough will be nice and soft and sticky. Place the ball back in the mixing bowl, drizzle with 2 teaspoons of olive oil, and roll the ball so that it's greased on all sides. Cover with plastic wrap and let the dough sit for 2 hours.

3. Cut the dough into 12 2-ounce pieces, then roll them into balls. Let them rest on a sheet pan dusted with flour and cover them with plastic wrap. Get your grill hot or if baking preheat your oven to 500 degrees.

4. Flour up a cutting board. Using a rolling pin, roll each ball into 7-inch circles (you're looking for ⅟₁₆-inch thickness).

5. Grill until you get good char marks (about a minute on each side) or bake each bread for 45 seconds on each side, or until you have nice brown blistering. Serve immediately.

Beverage
Unibroue,
Blanche De
Chambly

Soundtrack
"Strangers,"
The Kinks

Got Thyme?
make your own za'atar

This may be our desert-island spice. We can't name another dry rub that stretches so far. It's a complex war of herb, seed, and berry—a color jumble of combat-green, fire-flare pink, and a dotting of sesame-white. Drown it in a pool of extra virgin olive oil, and you have something akin to a chimichurri. To make za'atar at home is just to dump and stir from your spice cabinet. Mix 2 tablespoons dried thyme leaves, 1 tablespoon of dried oregano and/or marjarom, and 2 tablespoons toasted sesame seeds. Smash half of this mixture in a mortar and pestle, then recombine for a varied texture. Toss all this with 1 tablespoon of ground sumac and some salt. Put on everything, all the time.

Weed Dip Ⓥ

Serves 8 to 10

When we set out to make our imitation of the classic spinach-artichoke dip, we wanted to replace the greasy fondue-goo that chain restaurants pass off as four-cheese cream sauce with a lemon-herb coconut milk concoction. And since LA farmers markets bust with bunches of lamb's quarter in spring, we're always looking for uses of this military-green weed that is not only cheap (a buck a bag) but healthier than kale. Taken raw, the furry little leaves taste a little like dirty grass. Sautéed, they gain a nice buttery and vegetal richness that reminds us of both artichoke and creamed spinach—making the weed a perfect substitute for a dip that needs both. The only downside to serving this fake-cream, fake-artichoke dip at parties is that we usually end up standing next to the casserole dish all night explaining its conceit to every person who asks. Inevitably friends will furrow their brows and ask "why bother replacing the two vegetables?"—until that is, they dip to trip and see for themselves.

1 ½ cups cashews, raw
2 cups filtered water
1 tablespoon olive oil
1 sweet onion, diced
4 cloves garlic, minced
4 cups lamb's quarter, leaves only
1 can coconut milk

5 large basil leaves (½ cup of dill or oregano works)
2 teaspoons fresh lemon juice
half a nutmeg, grated
¼ cup breadcrumbs
1 tablespoon dried oregano
1 teaspoon onion powder
sea salt and fresh black pepper

1. Soak the cashews for at least 10 hours: dump them in a bowl and cover with filtered water, leave this on the counter with a clean towel covering it.

/////////// **10 Hours Later** ///////////

2. Prepare your lamb's quarter by plucking the leaves off whole from their stems. This can be time-consuming, so do it before starting to cook. Once you have 4 cups of leaves plucked, wash them and spin dry. Set aside.

3. Put a large saucepan on medium heat for a minute, adding olive oil. Toss in the diced sweet onion and minced garlic and cook for 5 minutes, stirring frequently to keep from browning. Now add half the lamb's quarter and stir. Let the leaves cook down substantially before adding the other half. Let cook for another 8 to 10 minutes. There should be little liquid but the leaves should be limp liked sautéed spinach. Add torn basil at the end of this period.

4. Add coconut milk to the pan and stir. Cook until the mixture hits a rolling boil, about 5 minutes, and turn down the flame to low. Simmer for up to 10 more minutes. Taste and season to your liking with sea salt and black pepper.

5. Drain your cashews and place them in a blender or food processor.

6. Once the pot has had time to simmer, carefully remove about half of the mixture from the bowl, using tongs and a ladle to get plenty of the cooked leaves, and add this to the blender with the soaked cashews. Puree this for several minutes until smooth and creamy. Return the puree to the pot.

7. Add the lemon juice and taste, adjusting seasoning as needed, and remove from heat. Pour this mixture into a casserole dish (or other oven-safe flat-bottomed container that is pretty enough you're not embarrassed to serve from it). Let this cool on the counter.

8. Mix together breadcrumbs and spices. Once the dip has cooled, evenly distribute the breadcrumb topping. Cover and refrigerate for at least an hour and up to a day.

9. To serve, drizzle additional olive oil on the top and put the dip under the broiler for 2 minutes to brown the breadcrumbs.

Beverage

Hollister, Pocket Full o' Green

Soundtrack

"Insane in the Brain," Cypress Hill

Lemon Sun Sandwich

Makes 2 sandwiches

The grilled cheese, one of childhood's simplest oral pleasures post-teet, has undergone a gourmet update, in which most chefs take a "more is more" approach. We think sometimes "more" is way too much. A wedge of Lemon Sun is the kind of sandwich you can balance between two fingers while nursing a mimosa. The grainy, slightly gamey, mouth gob that is melted Spanish sheep's cheese needs nothing more than a hit of sea salt and the lift of some puckery lemon-oil. It's not only light enough to eat in a sundress without feeling like an ogre, it also threatens none of the oily spills that jammed-full chef sandwiches typically end in. Our vegan version can't match the funk of real curds, but it will make your day if you're cheese-free.

4 slices of brioche (or other thick white bread)
4 ounces caña de oveja (or cashew "cream cheese")
2 tablespoons butter or margarine
1 tablespoon olive oil
zest of one lemon
1 teaspoon sea salt

1. If using butter, remove from the fridge and let sit out for 1 hour (or gently heat) to soften. While you wait, combine lemon zest and olive oil in a bowl and let sit.

2. To assemble sandwiches, spread butter evenly on one side of each bread slice, reserving half the butter for the pan. Slice the cheese into six equal-sized discs and dividing between the two sandwiches place the discs on non-buttered side. Sprinkle salt on the cheese and with a spoon carefully glaze with lemon oil. Close the sandwich with the second slice of bread, buttered side up.

3. Place a large skillet or cast-iron on high heat for a couple minutes, drop the rest of the butter on the skillet where you'll be grilling, and turn down to medium heat. Place sandwiches butter-side down in the pan and use a soup pot or similar object to press the sandwiches down. Cook this way for 2 minutes and check for color (you want light browning) as well as signs the cheese is melting.

4. Flip sandwiches and let cook until the cheese is oozing.

//////////

HEY YOU!

It's ideal to cut this cheese with a Roquefort bow, but if you're ill-equipped to deal with cheese properly (for shame) use dental floss (preferably un-minted).

//////////

Beverage
Hair of the Dog, Ruth

Soundtrack
"April Skies,"
Jesus and
Mary Chain

Cashew "Cream Cheese"

Makes 2 ¼ cups

2 cups raw cashews
1 ½ cups filtered water
1 teaspoon white miso
1 teaspoon Marmite
½ teaspoon nutmeg
⅓ cup fresh lemon juice
¼ cup grapeseed oil
sea salt to taste

1. The day before you need the cream cheese, put the cashews in a container with a lid, cover with water, and set it for 6 to 10 hours on the counter.

//////// The Next Day ////////

2. Drain the cashews and toss out the water. In a food processor, combine the soaked cashews with all ingredients except grapeseed oil. Pulse and slowly drizzle the oil. Let the mixture continue to blend several minutes, until it's thoroughly creamy and warm from the motor. Taste and season with salt as you like it.

Seedy Spears Ⓥ

Serves 8 to 10

Quinoa and asparagus are both ubiquitous delicacies that are frequently mishandled. Both are seemingly unfuckupable—yet both are often cursed to a fate of sludgery and limptitude by the heavy-handed cook. Quinoa is inherently snappy and nutty—so is asparagus—and we worked all our angles to come up with a process that consistently renders both irrevocably crunchy and bright. A 24-hour soaking in lemon brine belays any shrinkage in the asparagus, and a boil plus steam technique cooks the quinoa perfectly without it turning to goo. Add a fistful of herbs and some good olive oil and this will be your new repeat offender for any group food situation.

2 bunches asparagus
2 lemons, juiced
2 cups red quinoa
1 cup pistachio meat
1 bunch chives
1 cup dill, picked

1 bunch red bok choy
  (or green bok choy)
4 tablespoons olive oil
3 teaspoons sea salt
2 teaspoons Maldon salt
fresh black pepper to taste

Beverage

Marble Brewing,
Imperial Red

Soundtrack

"The Last Living
Rose," PJ Harvey

1. The day before you're serving, combine the juice of 1 lemon with 3 cups of water and 3 teaspoons of sea salt, and stir until the salt dissolves. Place this brine in a shallow container.

2. Trim the woody ends off your asparagus spears (if you bend them around the last half-inch they should break on their own). With a vegetable peeler, skin them—you don't have to get every little bit of skin off, just most of it. Submerge the asparagus in the brine and let it rest for several hours or overnight in your fridge.

/////////// **The Next Day** ///////////

3. Bring a large pot of salted water to a rolling boil and add the quinoa. Cover and cook for 10 minutes on high heat. After 10 minutes, use a fine mesh metal strainer to strain the quinoa over another sizable pot—you'll want most of that hot water for the next step. Leave the quinoa in the strainer.

4. Even the quinoa out on the bottom of the strainer and then carefully cover the strainer with two clean dishtowels, making sure that the entire strainer is covered with cloth. Bunch the bottom of the towels inside the top of the pot you strained most of the water into—make sure that the water level is at least 2 inches

below the bottom of the strainer when plugged on top of the pot. Return the water to a boil and steam the quinoa for 15 minutes. Remove from heat, and cool on a sheet pan.

5. Toast the pistachios on a sheet pan at 250 degrees for 10 minutes, or until you can smell the nuts. Remove and cool.

6. If using an outdoor grill to cook asapargus, fire it up. If cooking on stove get a cast-iron hot. Strain the spears from their brine and toss on and grill or stove for 2 minutes untouched, then roll each spear slightly to sear on the opposite sides of each. Grill for another 2 minutes and remove.

7. To serve, slice the grilled asparagus into quarter-inch pieces and combine with the quinoa, pistachios, olive oil, remaining lemon juice, diced dill, chopped chives, and julienned bok choy. Garnish with Maldon salt.

Beverage

Cantillon, Blubar

Soundtrack

"Godstar (California Mix)," Psychic TV

Fancy-Ass White Rice

Serves 6

Likely the most consumed foodstuff on the planet, rice rarely gets time to show off—especially in the summer time. This recipe finds its foundation in some pretty pricey grains—Acquerello Carnaroli—which are widely regarded as the best on the planet. The rice is aged untouched for one year before being processed in an esoteric machine called "the screw," which hulls and bleaches the rice purely by the grains rubbing against each other, dry humping them to tooth-colored perfection. You can try this dish with other types of rice, but the results won't be the same. Huge, unbreakable grains of flavorful rice are unmistakably remarkable with good olive oil, some ewe's milk feta, citrus, and lavender flowers.

////////

HEY YOU!

Seriously? You guys want me to by rice for $15 per pound? Yes. Yes we do. Get over it.

////////

    2 cups Acquerello Carnaroli
    8 ounces feta (preferably ewe's milk)
    2 grapefruit
    1 clementine
    1 tablespoon lavender flowers
    3 tablespoons extra virgin olive oil
    1 tablespoon ground black pepper
    half a cup of parsley leaves
    1 bunch chives

1. Heat a large pot of salted water (about 3 quarts) to boil. While it heats, crumble the feta and mince your herbs. Then supreme the grapefruit by carefully cutting the fruit sections out of their pith. Do the same with your clementine. (See page 108 for details on how to supreme citrus.)

2. Add the rice to the boiling water and cook uncovered for 15 minutes. Pretend you're making pasta. After 15, check one of the grains; there should be no snap in the center. When the rice is cooked through, strain it, rinse it, dry it, and toss with the olive oil while still warm.

3. Combine rice with the crumbled feta, herbs, fruit segments, and lavender flowers. Serve still warm.

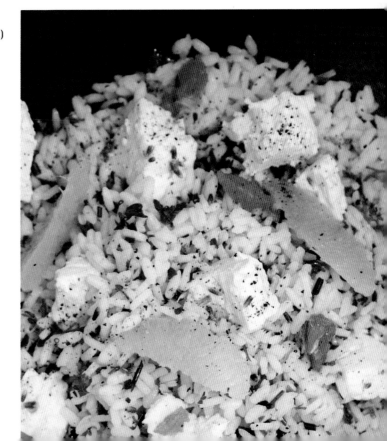

Spring Dresses

WHEN ALL YOU WANT to chomp on are butter lettuces, red leaf tangles, or romaine hearts, you're still gonna need something to gussy 'em up. Spicy, creamy, tangy, herbal—go hard or go home when it comes to dressings. We wanna feel it!

Cool Ranch

Makes about a cup

- ½ cup labneh (Greek yogurt works)
- ½ cup organic buttermilk
- 2 tablespoons fresh chives, minced
- 2 tablespoons fresh parsley, minced
- 1 tablespoon fresh dill, minced
- 1 teaspoon lemon zest
- 1 teaspoon paprika
- 1 ½ teaspoons sea salt
- 1 teaspoon fresh cracked black pepper
- ½ teaspoon agave syrup

1. Measure the labneh and buttermilk and combine by whisking in a cup.

2. Measure out herbs, spices, and zest and arrange in a large bowl.

3. Slowly pour the wet ingredients into the bowl and whisk to combine. Let sit for a few minutes to marry. Keeps for up to 3 days covered in the fridge.

Summer Sweater Ⓥ

Makes ¼ cup

- 2 habanero chiles
- 6 cloves garlic
- 2 scallions
- 4 teaspoons fresh oregano
- 2 tablespoons grapeseed oil
- 2 teaspoons orange zest
- 4 tablespoons orange juice
- ½ teaspoon sea salt

1. Mince the habanero, garlic, oregano, and scallions. Heat a skillet on high heat for about a minute.

2. Add the minced herbs and chile and toast for about 45 seconds, shaking often. Crush these toasties in a mortar and pestle to release their oils.

3. Combine the toasted herbs and chile with grapeseed oil, orange zest, and juice. Salt to taste.

Seizure Dressing Ⓥ

Makes 1 ½ cups

- 2 shiitake mushrooms
- 1 teaspoon white miso paste
- 4 tablespoons filtered water
- 4 tablespoons fresh lemon juice
- 1 teaspoon tahini
- 3 cloves garlic
- 2 teaspoons Wooster Sauce
- 1 quarter avocado
- 2 tablespoons plus one teaspoon grapeseed oil
- 2 tablespoons olive oil
- 1 tablespoon nutritional yeast
- ½ teaspoon white pepper
- Sea salt and black pepper to taste

1. Thinly slice the mushrooms and sauté on medium heat with a teaspoon of grapeseed oil for about 5 minutes, or until browning. Remove from heat and add the water to pan followed by miso to form a broth; shake or stir to dissolve.

2. Squeeze your lemon and measure out juice. Combine with tahini, garlic, Wooster Sauce, and avocado in a blender.

3. Pulse the mixture while slowly adding remaining grapeseed oil, followed by olive oil. Remove the shrooms from the broth (eat them now or reserve for salad) and drizzle in broth while pulsing. Add extra water if it its too thick for your liking. Taste and add salt and black pepper as desired.

Tomato Vinaigrette Ⓥ

Makes ½ cup

- 2 large ripe tomatoes
- 1 tablespoon white wine vinegar
- 2 tablespoons extra virgin olive oil
- 2 sprigs fresh tarragon, chopped
- 1 teaspoon sea salt
- fresh cracked black pepper to taste

1. Juice the tomatoes by rubbing on a handheld grater over a wide bowl while holding tight to the skin. Once all that remains is the peel, discard it.

2. Combine the vinegar and tarragon with the tomato juice. Whisk while drizzling in the olive oil. Season to taste.

Sweets

WE BOTH BLEED WHEN WE FLOSS AND ALEX HAS A COUPLE OF GOLD caps in his grill, but we can't blame our dental woes on a sweet tooth—neither of us has one. We get most of our calories from carbohydrates poured into pint glasses. **Sometimes we forget sugar even exists**.

But summer is the one time of year that we set aside our salt-and-oil hankerings and make room for glucose. **We like sugar highs from fresh fruit, saps, and fermented goo.** The rush can come from things as simple as inhaling chilled berries with fresh herbs, or as involved as cooking down a handful of overripe stone fruits with a long splash of liquor and then piping the entire hot mess into a homemade Pop-Tart. Sweet fixes may be come enrobed in fat from tree oils, smothering coconut custard, or encased in a pastry the color of way too much butter. But no matter how we take 'em, they can always be worked off with one simple exercise: lift one leg, leap onto several friends, and crowd surf into a keg stand. Repeat as necessary.

Ice Cream

Makes about 1 quart

There's a time and place for real cream and fresh eggs...and that place is inside our splintered wooden ice cream churn, cradled in the lap of one of our beautiful friends on a Sunday afternoon in July. Hand-churning ice cream is not only a rad party trick that makes anyone who touches the crank feel they've been teleported to a 1960s Michigan lake house; it's an insane upper-body workout. It also makes better ice cream. Two of these dream creams help feed our Weber Grill obsession: grilled peach and toasted corn make for frozen custards that deliver the essence of a cookout in an ice cream cone. All of these work in an electric ice cream maker, though why not take advantage of the rare chance to sentence your party guests to manual labor?

ICE CREAM BASE
1 cup heavy cream
3 cups half and half
1 cup white sugar
4 large egg yolks

1. Combine the various bovine juices in a medium saucepan and heat on high flame until just before it boils; when the sides sizzle, and the surface is undulating, turn off the heat.

2. Whip the yolks into the sugar until thoroughly combined; color will turn pale yellow.

3. In single cup increments, very slowly incorporate the hot milk into the eggy sugar mix, whisking gently. When everybody's all mixed, dump the combination back into the pot, and reheat on medium heat. (If you are making a flavored ice cream, you'll add the flavor element now.) Stir this custard with a wooden spoon until the mixture coats the back of the spoon and holds a line when you swipe your finger across. (Do not boil. Unless you want very creamy and sweet scrambled eggs.)

4. Once the base is properly warmed, place it in a heat-safe container, and chill in the fridge for at least 2 hours. Add to your ice cream maker of choice and process accordingly.

HEY YOU!

Gimme Friction! It's what makes cream, ice. If you're hand-cranking, go until the crank'll barely budge. If electric, make sure the arm component is dragging along the side, or you'll have milk soup.

Beverage

The Bruery, Oude Tart

Soundtrack

"Bewitched," Beat Happening

Toasted Corn

Makes 1 quart

    4 ears of corn, in husk
    4 limes, zested
    2 tablespoons red chile powder
    1 quart ice cream base (pg. 98)

1. If grilling, toss the unshucked ears of corn on the hot grill and put the lid on. Give them a quarter turn every 3 to 5 minutes until the outer husk is dry and toasted. Remove the ears and let cool. (If toasting in an oven, roast ears at 350 degrees for 8 to 10 minutes.)

2. Peel away the outer layers of husk and as much silk as you can. Place back on top of the grill to burn off extra silk. Leave the corn on the grill until about 70 percent of the kernels have browned slightly. (If toasting indoors, brown the ears on your stovetop burner.)

3. Slice off the kernels over a mixing bowl and reserve. Cut the cobs in half and put all of the corn bits in a medium saucepan with 1 quart of ice cream base custard (following instructions on pg. 98). Keep this all in same container when you chill it down. When you're ready to crank, leave kernels but make sure you remove the cobs.

4. Garnish with chile powder and lime zest.

Whiskey Cherry

Makes 1 quart

    1 pound fresh cherries
    ½ cup rye whiskey
    ¼ cup sugar
    1 quart ice cream base
       (pg. 98)

1. Pit the cherries: make a vertical slit on each and pop the pit out. (Wear a white T-shirt and you'll look really brutal later.)

2. Combine pitted cherries, whiskey, and sugar in a small saucepot and heat on high. Stir to incorporate. When it hits a boil, lower the flame and let simmer for 15 minutes.

3. Add mixture to ice cream base custard (following instructions on pg. 98). Then chill and spin.

Lemon Verbena

Makes 1 quart

    15 fresh lemon verbena leaves
    1 quart ice cream base (pg. 98)

1. Add the lemon verbena leaves to the milk and cream during the first step of making the ice cream custard (following instructions on pg. 98). Strain them out when mixing the custard base, and then add them back to the base when you chill the whole shebang down.

2. Puree the mixture in a blender to zap the steeped leaves into tiny bits. Crank yo' cream.

Grilled Peach

Makes 1 quart

    4 peaches (under-ripe)
    1 quart ice cream base (pg. 98)

1. Split peaches in half and place them skin down on a lightly oiled grill. Cook for 10 to 15 minutes, until the skin starts to blacken. Flip 'em and let them roast until there is a thin skin of carbon, about another 10 minutes. You don't just want grill marks; you want blackened fruit.

2. Let the peaches cool, then remove their pits and most of the charred exterior (leave some for flavor).

3. Roughly chop the peaches and add them to the ice cream base custard (following instructions on pg. 98). For smooth cream, puree them into the mix before spinning. For chunks, puree only half.

Summer Babe Sorbets

THE PHRASE "EASY AS PIE" SHOULD BE TRANSMOGRIFIED TO "simple as sorbet." Compare the steps, ingredients, and brainpower for the following recipes to the litany of laminated dough a few pages down. And you barely have to turn on your stove to make these ripping desserts. Heads up vegans: you ought never again be burned by base imitations of Ben & Jerry's. Call a spade a spade: frozen coconut milk is still sorbet (and these are better than all of them phonies).

Persian Cuke Ⓥ

Makes 1 quart

> 4 cups water
> 4 cups white sugar
> 6 Persian cucumbers

1. Make a simple syrup. Combine sugar and water in a medium-sized pot. Crank the heat and bring to a boil, whisking to dissolve the sugar. After it hits a boil, turn it off.

2. Wash and roughly chop your cukes. Add half of them to a blender or food processor. Add just enough syrup to make the mixture move, and then puree till kingdom come. Repeat with the rest, then combine and mix the syrup with the puree in a container with a lid. Chill the mix down overnight (or until cold).

3. To use, pour the chilled mix over a fine mesh strainer and into a bowl, using a ladle or spatula to press the liquid through. Process the strained mix in an ice cream maker of your choice. Garnish with a sprinkle of salt and a squeeze of lemon.

Strawberry Hibiscus Ⓥ

Makes 1 quart

> 4 cups of water
> 4 cups of white sugar
> 2 tablespoons dried hibiscus
> 2 baskets of strawberries

1. Make a simple syrup. Combine sugar and water in a medium-sized pot. Crank the heat and bring to a boil, whisking to dissolve the sugar. After it hits a boil, turn it off.

2. Add the hibiscus to simple syrup and stir to incorporate, letting it steep while you prep your berries.

3. De-stem and wash those berries. Halve them. Add half of them to a blender or food processor. Add just enough syrup to make the mixture move, and then puree till kingdom come. Repeat with the rest, combine and mix the syrup with the puree in a container with a lid. Chill the mix down overnight (or until cold).

4. To use, pour the chilled mix over a fine mesh strainer and into a bowl, using a ladle or spatula to press the liquid through. Process the strained mix in an ice cream maker of your choice. Garnish with saba or a drizzle of olive oil.

Icey Hot Ⓥ

Makes 1 quart

> 6 poblano chiles
> 6 Anaheim chiles
> 4 cups water
> 4 cups white sugar

1. Burn the shit out of your chiles over an open flame. A grill is best, but your stove top works. Cook them until every inch of skin is black, rotating them often to evenly disperse the heat. As they finish blackening, toss them in a paper bag to cool.

2. Make a simple syrup. Combine sugar and water in a medium-sized pot. Crank the heat and bring to a boil, whisking to dissolve the sugar. After it hits a boil, turn it off.

3. When the chiles are cool enough to handle, rub off the charred skins. Make a vertical incision on each pepper and remove all the seeds and connective membranes (skip this if you want a spicier sorbet). Add half of them to a blender or food processor with just enough syrup to make the mixture move, and then puree till kingdom come. Repeat with the rest, combine and mix the syrup with the puree in a container with a lid. Chill the mix down overnight (or until cold).

4. To use, pour the chilled mix over a fine mesh strainer and into a bowl, using a ladle or spatula to press the liquid through. Process the strained mix in an ice cream maker of your choice. Garnish with a shot of tequila or mezcal.

Booze Holes Ⓥ

Named for their shape as well as what it feels like when you eat too many, booze holes fall somewhere in between liqueur truffles and donut holes. We first learned to love eating booze when we made a vegan adaptation to the Southern classic, bourbon balls. The first bite tastes like Granny's baking cupboard, but as soon as you breathe out, the unmistakable sting of bourbon whistles on your throat. This recipe, at its core, is just cookie crumbs, roasted nuts, and powdered sugar all made wet and sticky with a mixture of booze and syrup. This allows you to play baker and bartender at the same time, so you can stumble (literally, you will fall) upon combinations limited only by the span of your wet bar and your spice rack.

The basic recipe for booze holes is below; ingredients for specific types of boozy cakes follows.

Beverage

Schloss
Eggenberg,
Samichlaus Bier

Soundtrack

"There is a Light
That Never
Goes Out,"
The Smiths

1. Roast your nuts. Crank your oven to 325 degrees. In a sauce pot, gently heat the margarine until melted (but not spitting). Add all spices for the nuts and stir until distributed.

2. In a large mixing bowl, toss the nuts with the spiced margarine until evenly coated. Slide the whole mess onto a baking sheet and bake for about 20 minutes, shaking every 5 or so to keep from burning. Remove once roasted and let cool for at least 10 minutes before using.

3. Prepare the "dough." In a mixing bowl, sift 1 cup of the powdered sugar (don't buy a sifter, duh, just slowly pour the sugar over a fine mesh strainer and shake it over your bowl till it's all pillowy).

4. Dump your cool nuts on a cutting board and go to town, roughly chopping them into bits. Add this to the mixing bowl.

5. In a separate bowl, whisk the syrup (molasses or agave) and ¼ cup of booze, until evenly married. Take the extra shot for good measure! Now add this goo to the bowl of sugary nuts.

6. Put the vanilla wafers (use HK Vanilla Wafers, pg. 105, or store-bought cookies work too) in a food processor and pulse them to shit. (You want a fine dust of cookie crumbs.) Add the wafer crumbs to the mixture and use a spatula to mix it all together.

7. Place the leftover powdered sugar on a plate with zest or coconut for topping. Begin pinching the mixed dough into ball shapes, about the diameter of a quarter. Press together with enough pressure to make the dough stick, then roll into a ball using both palms. Form one at a time and roll them in extra sugar topping. Repeat until the bowl is empty. Refrigerate for 30 minutes before eating.

Pastis

Makes about 30

PISTACHIOS
1 cup pistachios
2 tablespoons margarine
1 teaspoon sea salt

DOUGH
2 cups vanilla wafer dust
1 ¼ cup powdered sugar
2 tablespoon agave
¼ cup pastis, plus one shot
½ teaspoon sea salt
¼ cup lemon zest

Gin

Makes about 30

CASHEWS
1 cup cashews
2 tablespoons margarine
2 tablespoons ground cardamom
1 teaspoon sea salt

DOUGH
2 cups vanilla wafer dust
1 ¼ cup powdered sugar
2 tablespoon agave
¼ cup gin, plus one shot
½ teaspoon sea salt
¼ cup finely shredded coconut
¼ cup lime zest

continued on page 105

Mezcal

Makes about 30

SEEDED ALMONDS
¾ cup almonds
¼ cup pepitas
2 tablespoons margarine
2 tablespoons ground cumin
1 teaspoon habanero powder
1 teaspoon sea salt

DOUGH
2 cups vanilla wafer dust
1 ¼ cup powdered sugar
2 tablespoon agave
¼ cup mezcal, plus one shot
½ teaspoon sea salt
¼ cup orange and lime zest

Bourbon

Makes about 30

PECANS
1 cup pecans
2 tablespoons margarine
2 tablespoons smoked paprika
1 teaspoon mace (nutmeg works)
1 teaspoon smoked salt
1 teaspoon cayenne pepper
½ teaspoon cinnamon
½ teaspoon sea salt

DOUGH
2 cups vanilla wafer dust
1 ¼ cup powdered sugar
2 tablespoons raw cocoa
2 tablespoons molasses
¼ cup bourbon, plus one shot
½ teaspoon sea salt

HK Vanilla Wafers Ⓥ

Makes a dozen (About 2 cups cookie dust)

½ cup margarine
1 cup white sugar
2 tablespoons "vanilla vodka" (pg. 106)
1 ⅓ cups all-purpose flour
¾ teaspoon baking powder
½ teaspoon sea salt

Beverage

Brasserie
Dupont, Avril

Soundtrack

"Motorcrash,"
Sugarcubes

1. Crank the oven to 350 degrees.

2. Cream the margarine, sugar, and vanilla vodka in a mixing bowl. Sift the flour and all other dry ingredients into a separate bowl and mix. Then add this to the creamed ingredients and mix.

3. Drop the dough onto a lightly greased baking sheet, one teaspoon at a time, about 2 inches apart. Bake for about 15 minutes or until just starting to brown.

Vodka Magic
make your own vanilla extract

Is that little brown bottle of vanilla goodness empty? Make your own. Next time you're using vanilla beans for a recipe, don't throw away the long brown pods after you scrape 'em of their seedy guts—these spent pods will make you months of extract while saving you cash (and a trip to the spice shop). Just submerge them in the booze of your choice (we use Popov for scuzz factor, but you can use whatever: rum, whiskey, brandy). Store this spice flask at room temp and shake it every day for a week. Then it's ready to use and will keep indefinitely. Refill it at you use it, and keep adding spent pods and you'll never buy extract again.

Summer Fruit Salads

FRUIT SALAD. IT'S ONE OF THE SIMPLEST DISHES TO MAKE, and one of the most commonly reprehensible to eat. Generally if you're eating a medley of "fresh" fruit, it's a study in under- and overripeness, just to the left of a pile of hash-browns at one of those brunch spots you always find yourself going to, even though the food really isn't good. Alright, we'll get down from the soapbox. Lots of summer fruits have an incredibly short ripeness window, but done right they spruce up any spread. The perfect equation (fruit + aromatic = solid fruit salad) should become one that you memorize. Now do your homework and create some of your own.

Stonefruit and Strawberries ⓥ

Serves 12

- 6 nectarines
- 2 baskets (12 ounces) of strawberries
- 2 tablespoons fresh tarragon leaves
- 1 lemon, juiced
- 4 tablespoons honey
- 6 tablespoons olive oil

1. Core the nectarines by slicing them in half all the way around the pit. They should pull apart easily, but if they don't you can carefully cut around the pits and suffer a small amount of waste. Slice the pitted segments lengthwise into wedges and toss them in a mixing bowl with the lemon juice.

2. Wash, de-stem, and quarter the strawberries. Put them with the nectarines.

3. Using a fork, whisk the honey into the olive oil. (This won't form a perfect emulsion and that's ok.) Pour over the fruits. Garnish with tarragon and serve immediately.

Blue and Peaches ⓥ

Serves 4

- 8 doughnut peaches
- ½ cup plus 2 teaspoons water
- ½ cup sugar
- ½ teaspoon ginger powder
- ¼ cup blueberries
- 1 teaspoon kudzu starch
- 1 lime, zested

1. Heat the ½ cup water and sugar in a small saucepan until it boils. Stir to dissolve the sugar and add the ginger powder.

2. Add blueberries to the now bubbling syrup. Reduce the heat to low and cook for 15 minutes.

3. Remove from heat and smash the blueberries in the pan with a large spoon, or ladle. (Don't burn yourself with boiling sugar water.) Strain out the solids, and return the syrup to its pot.

4. In a separate bowl, dissolve the kudzu in the 2 teaspoons of water and mix out all the lumps with a fork. Add this slurry to the blueberry syrup and crank the heat back to high. Stir the sauce with a spoon until it thickens, about 3 minutes. Chill it.

5. Halve the doughnut peaches, pit 'em, and get architectural with your plating (pretending you're a dessert chef asshole). Garnish them with the blue sauce and lime zest.

Street Fruit ⓥ

Serves 8

- 1 pineapple
- 3 mangoes
- 1 small jicama
- 3 Persian cucumbers
- 2 grapefruit
- 3 oranges
- 2 teaspoons urfa biber (chile powder works)
- 1 teaspoon sea salt
- 1 cup cilantro leaves
- 4 limes, juiced

1. Skin the pineapple, jicama, and cucumber. Core the pineapple. Slice the cukes into quarter-inch disks, and cube the pineapple and jicama similarly.

2. Supreme the citrus. Don't know how? Slice the tops and bottoms off of each fruit, and then cut away the peel by carving around the curvature of each fruit—make sure you cut deep enough that there is no pith (white stuff) remaining. Hold a fruit in your hand and carefully cut a "V" in each segment, with the apex of the cut meeting a little before the core of the fruit. The supremed slices will slide right out. Do this over a bowl to catch all the precious juices, and squeeze the supremed fruit to wring out its life force.

3. Cut the mangoes as close to their pits as possible. Carefully cut a grid matrix into the tops and bottoms of the pieces with no pits while holding each piece in the palm of your hand. Use a spoon to scoop out the cubes you've made.

4. Combine all your fruits in a mixing bowl with lime, salt, cilantro, and urfa (or chile powder). Mix and serve immediately. To serve outdoors, place equal amounts of each fruit in plastic bags and shake to combine. Serve with plastic forks.

Pies: In Your Face

This one goes out to the Triple B (Biotic Baking Brigade), the vegan activists who have managed to smear Bill Gates, Rupert Murdoch, Anne Coulter, and multiple mayors of San Francisco with various animal-free pastry creams. While we wouldn't advocate turning these somewhat time-consuming sweets into clever missiles to smite the right wing, we make them as a salute to the time-honored tradition of public pieing.

Crustlord

Makes 2 eight-inch pie crusts, 8 Pop-Tarts, or 10 tartlet shells

- 2 ½ cups all-purpose flour
- 2 tablespoons sugar
- 1 teaspoon salt
- 8 ounces butter
- ½ cup water, plus more as needed
- ½ teaspoon apple cider vinegar

D-Beat Dough (V)

(Makes 2 eight-inch pie crusts, 8 Pop-Tarts, or 10 tartlet shells

- 2 ½ cups all-purpose flour
- 2 teaspoons sugar
- 2 teaspoons kosher salt
- 8 ounces Earth Balance vegan shortening
- ½ cup water, plus more as needed
- ½ teaspoon apple cider vinegar

1. Combine the dry goods in a mixing bowl, stir to combine, and put the bowl in the freezer. Blend the water and the vinegar and stash it in the freezer.

2. Cut your butter or shortening into tiny pieces. Your butter should have just come out the fridge. A Roquefort bow is the ideal tool, but a sharp knife will do. We generally go for teeny cubes, so stand your sticks of fat so they're vertical on a board, and quarter them top down, then dice the smaller sticks into wee cubes. Add the cubes to the freezing flour, and then place back in the freezer for 20 minutes.

3. Remove the chilled bowl of flour and fat, and using a pastry cutter or a large fork grind the already smallish cubes of lipid into smaller pieces. Pulverize the center of the bowl, then heap more flour and butter pieces on top. Do this until the mixture is approaching rice-sized fat and flour nuggets. This should take about 5 minutes of mixing. You don't need or want to fully incorporate the fat into the flour; if you can't see pieces of butter/margarine, you've overmixed. That's not the end of the world, but your cooked dough will have a less flaky texture.

4. Add the vinegar water. Use your hands to force the dough together. It will seem like there isn't enough liquid. Don't be deterred. Force the issue until everybody is jammed up together in a big buttery ball. Wrap tightly with plastic and refrigerate. For best results, wait until the next day to use the dough, but it's ready after sitting for at least an hour.

HEY YOU!

Don't second-guess Evan's mother-in-law. She's been tipping a cap of vinegar in her dough for years. Something about it lends a better taste and texture and we don't care why.

Beverage

Cismontane, Double Rainbow

Soundtrack

"Eat Cake," Free Kitten

Shaping
Pies, Pop-Tarts, Tartlets

Now that you're armed with a solid sweetcrust recipe, don't feel pinned down by the pie pan. Rethink the shape and structure, and pies can become more portable, personalized, and totally precious.

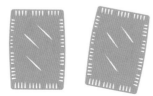

Pop-Tarts

Roll out one quarter a batch of dough (pg. 110) into an 18 x 6-inch strip that is a quarter-inch thick. Use a bench knife (or any knife) dipped in water to cut the dough into 6 x 3-inch rectangles. Place 4 tablespoons of filling in the center of one piece of dough, gently lay another piece on top, and then seal the edges by pressing with a fork. Dip the fork in water if it starts to stick. Trim the edges with the bench knife, and then slit a few diagonal vents along the top of the tart. Bake for 30 minutes, or until the dough is nice and golden. Transfer to a rack to cool and keep your hands to yourself. Eating these before they cool will do damage to that tongue of yours.

Tradish Big Boi

Take half a batch of dough (pg. 110) allotment of dough and roll it into a ball. Plop that sucker down on a floured work surface, coat your hands and a rolling pin with flour, and give the ball four solid rolls, making an oval shape. Turn the top of your oval counter clockwise to 10 o'clock and roll from the lower point forward, making a lopsided circle. Keep turning and rolling until you've got a circle of dough a quarter-inch thick. Flop this sucker atop a pie pan, and gently press the dough to the bottom and sides, folding the excess over the top rim of the pan. Use a sharp pair of scissors to trim off the extra dough, but leave about a quarter inch of overhang. Dimple this overhang into the edge of the pie pan with a fork. Add your filling, and bake for 40 minutes at 350, or until the crust is golden brown. Transfer to a rack to cool, and contain yourself. This needs to sit for at least 45 minutes for the filing to set.

Tartlets

If you have wee tart tins, good for you. If you don't, stick with Pop-Tarts. But if you do, roll out the dough like you would to make the Pop-Tarts, and slice squares that would more than cover your tart tins. Snip and shape as with the Tradish Big Boi pie, but on a small scale. Now prick the bottom of the dough. Place a small square of wax paper in the bottom of each tart, and put about ¼ cup of dry beans on the paper (if you have pie weights, now's the time to question their necessity). Bake the tart shells at 350 for 35 minutes or until golden brown. Remove and cool, then remove them from their tins and fill with coconut cream (see pg. 113) and fresh fruit pie.

Fillings ⓥ
Coconut Cream

Makes 8 to 10 tartlets

Beverage

Founders,
Barrel Aged
Porter

Soundtrack

"Runnin Down
a Dream,"
Tom Petty & the
Heartbreakers

Note: This sweet goo works best when it's not cooked; you'll want to add it to finished crusts and serve that way. You can try making a Pop-Tart, but don't blame us if it explodes.

2 cans coconut milk
½ cup sugar
2 tablespoons kudzu starch
2 tablespoons water

1. Combine the coconut milk and the sugar in a small sauce pot and stir to combine. Heat on medium heat.

2. Mix the kudzu starch and the water together until the kudzu dissolves. Add this to the coconut milk and stir. Keep the heat on; as the milk gets close to a boil it will start to thicken considerably. Like, a lot. Like, you'll be all confused at how thick it will get. Cool the mix down after it's approached pudding texture.

3. Get thee some tart shells and dollop to your heart's content. Garnish with fresh berries, or layer with Rumerized Pineapple to get all piña colada like.

Manhattan

Makes 1 large pie, 8 Pop-Tarts, or 8 to 10 tartlets

> 2 pounds cherries
> ¾ cup rye whiskey
> ¼ cup sweet vermouth
> ½ cup sugar
> zest of one orange
> Angostura Bitters

1. Pit the cherries. (For a refresher on technique and appropriate dress, see pg. 99).

2. Combine the pitted cherries, booze, and sugar in a medium pot and bring to a boil. Reduce heat to low and simmer for 20 minutes. Chill.

3. When shaping pies, zest the orange and distribute it evenly over the top of the filling. Dash two drops of bitters per square inch of exposed filling, finish shaping and bake as directed per shape.

 Beverage Kiuchi Brewery, Commemorative Ale   **Soundtrack** "Baby Blue," The Warlocks

Rumerized Pineapple

Makes enough for 8 to 10 tartlets

> 1 ripe pineapple
> 1 vanilla bean
> ½ cup rum
> 4 teaspoons butter
>   (or margarine), divided

1. Skin the pineapple, and slice into quarter-inch thick rounds. Preheat your oven to 350 degrees.

2. Heat a large skillet on medium-high flame and melt 1 tablespoon of butter. When butter is sizzling, add four to five slices of pineapple, depending on the size of your pan, and cook undisturbed for 5 minutes. Check for color—you want a good caramelization—then flip and sear the other side before removing. Repeat this process, adding more butter as needed until all your pineapple is cooked.

3. Split and scrape the vanilla bean (reserve spent pods for making vanilla extract) and whisk the seeds into the rum.

4. Load all the pineapple into a roasting dish, and add the vanilla rum. Braise at 350 for 25 minutes. Remove and cool and you're ready for pies.

 Beverage Ballast Point, Sour Wench   **Soundtrack** "No Fun," The Stooges

Oaxacan Apricot

Makes 1 large pie, 8 Pop-Tarts, or 8 to 10 tartlets

> 2 pounds fresh apricots
> 1 cup mezcal
>   (tequila will do)
> 1 cup sugar

1. Halve and pit the apricots, and combine in a medium saucepan with the booze and sugar. Heat on high and stir to combine.

2. Once the mix hits a bubble-boil, reduce heat to medium and simmer for 20 minutes, stirring frequently. Let the mix cool down a bit before adding to dough and shaping.

 Beverage Dogfish Head, Aprihop **Soundtrack** "Orange Skies," Love

Spiced Pecan Pie

Makes 1 large pie, 8 Pop-Tarts, or 8 to 10 tartlets

2 cups spiced pecans (below)
3 tablespoons flax seed meal
9 tablespoons water
4 tablespoons vegan
   margarine, melted
½ cup white sugar
½ cup brown sugar
1 cup brown rice syrup
1 ball D-Beat Dough (pg. 110)

Beverage

Allagash, Curieux

Soundtrack

"Knives of Summertime," Sparklehorse

1. Preheat oven to 325 degrees. Measure out the flax meal and combine with water in a bowl, letting it sit for several minutes to gel. In a mixing bowl, combine the sugars, the rice syrup, and the margarine.

2. Roll out your dough in desired shape (pg. 111) and prepare for filling.

3. Add the soaked flax meal and stir well. Mixture should be sticky but consistent throughout without clumps. Lastly add the pecans and stir just enough to distribute.

4. Carefully fill your pie crust with the filling, being sure not to fill higher than ⅔ up the height of the pie to avoid sugar boil-over. (If you have leftover goo, boo hoo. Eat it! Stays good in fridge for weeks.)

5. Bake pie in oven with a baking tray underneath for 45 to 50 minutes. Watch it closely after 30 minutes; if it rises and threatens spill-over, poke the surface with a chop stick to deflate. Once the crust is golden and the goo is starting to caramelize, remove from oven. Let sit until fully cool before serving.

Spiced Pecans (V)

2 cups pecans
¼ cup vegan margarine
2 tablespoons smoked paprika
1 teaspoon mace (nutmeg works)
1 teaspoon smoked salt
1 teaspoon cayenne pepper
½ teaspoon cinnamon
½ teaspoon sea salt

HEY YOU!

Our pecan filling makes an obnoxiously good Pop-Tart but all that sugar is a bit unstable. Fridge the filling overnight to set, and spoon mostly nuts, less goo into the tart, and don't freak if it leaks a little.

1. Roast your nuts. Crank your oven to 325 degrees. In a sauce pot, gently heat the margarine until melted (but not spitting). Add all spices for the nuts and stir until distributed.

2. In a large mixing bowl, toss the nuts with the spiced margarine until evenly coated. Slide the whole mess onto a baking sheet and bake for about 20 minutes, shaking every 5 or so to keep from burning. Remove once roasted and let cool for at least 10 minutes before using.

Evan George & Alex Brown

Evan George is a public radio producer and writer whose coverage of the health insurance industry, homelessness, and the federal court system has won local and national awards—none of which have stemmed from his extensive writing about beer, coffee, and cooking for publications including *Los Angeles* magazine, *Condé Nast Traveler*, and the *Los Angeles Times*. Born and raised outside of Washington, DC, George credits his formative high school years drinking beer in Berlin, Germany, for his love for strong suds. He has grilled steaks at a Philadelphia bistro, flipped burgers in LA coffee shops, and, most recently, spent three years as a sous chef at the renowned vegetarian hot spot Elf Cafe. He holds a history degree from Occidental College.

Alex Brown currently holds court as the general manager for Gourmet Imports, where he answers the questions, and tempers the fury, of the best chefs, cheesemongers, and restaurateurs in Los Angeles. He's an expert frequently quoted on cheese by food publications including *Imbibe*, the *LA Weekly*, and the *Los Angeles Times*. A long-standing line cook vet, Brown took his first cooking job at age 14 as dishwasher/prep cook/garde-manger at the now extinct Indigo Crow Bistro in Albuquerque, New Mexico. His innate obsession with ales began as a baby: his mother routinely drank Guinness Export prior to breastfeeding (thanks, Ma). When he's not importing obscure cheeses, sniffing truffles, vetting olive oils, or being a brute, he headbangs in the internationally renowned sludge band Robedoor, and is an avid lover of cycling.

🍾 HK Beer List

Alesmith Yulesmith (Summer Release) 57	**La Chouffe Houblon** 48
Allagash Curieux 115	**Ladyface Workers Cohopritive** 42
Anchor Humming 11	**Lagunitas Little Sumpin' Wild** 70
Ballast Point Sculpin IPA 23	**Left Hand Milk Stout** 85
Ballast Point Smoked Helles 54	**Lost Abbey Red Barn Ale** 81
Ballast Point Sour Wench 114	**Marble Brewing Imperial Red** 91
Bear Republic Hop Rod Rye 43	**Maui Brewing Flyin' HI.P.Hay** 44
Brasserie Dupont Avril 105	**Mikkeller Tomahawk** 13
Brewdog Tokyo 68	**New Belgian Clutch** 77
Cantillon Blubar 92	**North Coast Le Merle Saison** 83
Cismontane Double Rainbow 110	**North Coast Prankster** 73
Craftsman Fireworks Saison 69	**Odell Double Pilsner** 55
Craftsman Sour Braggot 24	**Ommegang Hennepin** 37
Deschutes Black Butte Porter 34	**Oskar Blues Mama's Little Yella Pils** 64
Deschutes Mirror Mirror 59	**Oskar Blues Old Chub** 31
Dogfish Head Aprihop 114	**Rogue Dad's Little Helper Black IPA** 62
Eagle Rock Populist 22	**Russian River Pliny the Elder** 71
Eagle Rock Solidarity 12	**Schloss Eggenberg Samichlaus Bier** 103
Firestone Walker Pale 31 19	**Sierra Nevada Foam** 30
Firestone Walker Velvet Merlin 17	**St. Sebastiaan Yeast Hoist** 32
Founders Barrel Aged Porter 113	**Stone Levitation Ale** 41
Goose Island Bourbon County Stout 33	**Stone Ruination** 38
Great Divide Belgian Imperial Stout 83	**Telegraph Reserve Wheat** 49
Green Flash Double Stout 32	**The Bruery Gunga Galunga** 63
Green Flash West Coast IPA 11	**The Bruery Oude Tart** 98
Hair of the Dog Ruth 90	**Unibroue Blanche De Chambly** 86
Hollister Pocket Full o' Green 87	**Victory Prima Pils** 76
Jolly Pumpkin Bam Noir 84	**Weihenstephaner 1809** 25
Kern River Just Outstanding IPA 58	
Kiuchi Brewery Commemorative Ale 114	

▣ HK Playlist

Al Green: "Here I Am," from *Call Me* (Hi Records, 1972), 11

Alien Sex Fiend: "Burger Bar Baby," from *Curse* (Anagram Records, 1990), 58

Band of Bees: "Sky Holds the Sun," from *Sunshine Hit Me* (Astralwerks, 2003), 30

Beat Happening: "Bewitched," from *Jamboree* (K Records/Rough Trade Records, 1988), 98

Black Flag: "Six Pack" from *Six Pack* (SST Records, 1981), 42

Brian Jonestown Massacre: "Ballad of Jim Jones" from *thank god for mental illness* (Bomp! Records, 1996), 34

Chairlift: "Amanaemonesia" from *Something* (Columbia Records, 2012), 32

Comets on Fire: "Pussy Foot the Duke" from *Blue Cathedral* (Sub Pop, 2004), 54

Cuticle: "Merciful Sword" from *Merciful Sword* (100% Silk, 2011), 83

Cypress Hill: "Insane in the Brain" from *Black Sunday* (Ruffhouse, 1993), 87

David Bowie: "Rebel, Rebel," from *Diamond Dogs* (RCA Records, 1974), 68

Dinosaur Jr.: "Kracked" from *You're Living All Over Me* (SST Records, 1987), 41

Echo and the Bunnymen: "The Killing Moon" from *Ocean Rain* (Korova, 1984), 55

Frank Black: "Los Angeles" from *Frank Black* (4AD, 1993), 19

Free Kitten: "Eat Cake" from *Sentimental Education* (Kill Rock Stars, 1997), 110

Gang of Four: "Damaged Goods" from *Entertainment* (EMI, 1979), 31

Glass Candy: "Love on a Plate" from *Love Love Love* (Troubleman Unlimited Records, 2003), 17

Jesus and Mary Chain: "April Skies" from *Darkland* (Blanco y Negro, 1987), 90

Le Tigre: "Decepticon (DFA remix)" from *DFA Remixes* (DFA Records, 2006), 29

Lee Scratch Perry: "Bionic Rats" from *Soundzs From The Hot Line* (Heartbeat Records, 1992), 77

Lionel Hampton: "On Green Dolphin Street" from *Soft Vibes Soaring Strings* (Columbia Records, 1961), 83

Lou Reed: "I'm So Free" from *Transformers* (RCA Records, 1972), 33

Loudon Wainright III: "The Swimming Song" from *Attempted Mustache* (Columbia Records, 1973), 49

Love: "Orange Skies" from *Da Capo* (Elektra Records, 1967), 114

Ministry: "Jesus Built My Hotrod" from *Psalm 69* (Sire, 1992), 25

My Morning Jacket: "Outta My System" from *Circuital* (ATO, 2011), 48

Nirvana: "Ain't It a Shame" from *With the Lights Out* (DGC, 2004), 71

Pavement: "Range Life" from *Crooked Rain, Crooked Rain* (Matador, 1994), 76

PJ Harvey: "The Last Living Rose" from *Let England Shake* (Island, 2011), 91

Primal Scream: "Suicide Sally and Jonny Guitar" from *Riot City Blues* (Sony Records, 2006), 64

Psychic TV: "Godstar (California Mix)" from *Godstar* (Temple Records, 1985), 92

Pulp: "Babies" from *His n' Hers* (Island, 1994), 63

Randy Newman: "I Love LA" from *Trouble in Paradise* (Warner Bros., 1983), 22

Redbone: "Drinkin' and Blo" from *Potlatch* (Epic, 1970), 24

Scotty: "Draw Your Brakes" from *Draw Your Brakes* (Crystal, 1972), 73

Selda: "Mehmet Emmi" from *Selda* (Türküola, 1976), 84

Shit Robot: "Triumph!!!" from *From the Cradle to the Rave* (DFA, 2010), 59

Singapore Sling: "Summer Garden" from *The Curse of Singapore Sling* (Stinky, 2002), 57

Sparklehorse: "Knives of Summertime" from *Dreamt For Light Years in the Belly of a Mountain* (Astralwerks, 2006), 115

Sugarcubes: "Motorcrash" from *Life's too Good* (Elektra, 1988), 105

T. Rex: "Raw Ramp" from *Electric Warrior* (Reprise, 1971), 70

Taj Mahal: "Bacon Fat" from *Giant Step…* (Columbia Records, 1969), 43

Talking Heads: "This Must be the Place" from *Speaking in Tongues* (Sire, 1983), 81

The Clash: "Spanish Bombs" from *London Calling* (CBS, 1979), 23

The Cramps: "The Mad Daddy" from *Songs the Lord Taught Us* (Illegal Records, 1980), 62

The Cure: "Fire in Cairo" from *Three Imaginary Boys* (Fiction, 1979), 12

The Kinks: "Strangers" from *Lola Versus Powerman and the Monkeygoround, Part One* (Pye, 1970), 86

The Make Up: "White Belts" from *Save Yourself* (K Records, 1999), 11

The Misfits: "Hollywood Babylon" from *Bullet* (Plan 9 Records, 1978), 13

The Rentals: "Barcelona" from *Seven More Minutes* (Reprise, 1999), 44

The Smiths: "There is a Light That Never Goes Out" from *The Queen is Dead* (Rough Trade, 1986), 103

The Stooges: "No Fun" from *No Fun* (Elektra, 1969), 114

The Warlocks: "Baby Blue" from *Phoenix EP* (Birdman Records, 2002), 114

Tom Petty and the Heartbreakers: "Runnin Down a Dream" from *Full Moon Fever* (MCA, 1989), 113

U2 Featuring Johnny Cash: "The Wanderer" from *Zooropa* (Isalnd, 1993), 32

Valet: "Fire" from *The Second Marriage Records Compilation* (Marriage Records, 2008), 85

We Are the World: "Clay Stones" from *Clay Stones* (Manimal Vinyl, 2010), 38

White Rainbow: "Sun Shadow Drifter" from *Sky Drips Drifts* (States Rights Records, 2007), 37

YACHT: "Summer Song" from *See Mystery Lights* (DFA, 2009), 69

Index

Tortillas
  Ambient Nachos, 25, 37
  Jackfruit Carnitas, 13-14

 **V**

Vanilla Extract, 106

 **W**

Walnuts
  Malted Muhamarra, 84
Watermelon-Strawberry Aguas Frescas,
  16
Weekends and parties, 2-3
Wieners
  HK Dogs, 54
  Hobo Franks & Beans, 34
Wild Grub, 8, 27-38
Wormseed (epazote), 23, 24

Z

Za'atar, 86

Acknowlegments

Alex and Evan would like to thank anyone and everyone we've ever had the pleasure to spoon-feed, pour a drink, or scromp with on a summer picnic blanket.

Endless, drunken praise and IOUs go to Jen Wick and Aaron Farley, with extra beer hugs to Chris, Sage, Buzz, Christopher and Jake, Brandi Bowles and Foundry, Renée Sedliar and everyone at Da Capo.

Evan swears his thanks up and down to Meagan for everything. Thanks Carol for pie advice. And mad props to Cindy and Roger for letting me man the grill early and often.

Alex would be one sorry sucker were it not for the mesmerizing magnetism of his lady love: thanks Lake. Love to all my Families; blood, sweat, and otherwise.

Hearty, gut-bomb Thank You's to all who ate food for this book:

Lake Sharp, Meagan Yellott, Ali Hyman, Mike Meanstreets, Ian Hughes, Christina Paul, Emily Wilder, Evan Nicoll-Johnson, Clara Iwasaki, Greg and Erica (and young Jude) Buss, Michele Johnson, Russell Dykann, Todd Walker, Kimberly Reiss, Cord Jefferson, Chris Martins, Annie O'Malley, Scott Zweisen, Jonny Smith, Colin and Daine Blodorn, Baine and Dara Kerr, Jason Weiner, Dave Stickel, Alex Macy, Spencer Jackson, Tucker Neel, Sean Klaseus, Adele Jaques, Michael Dunn, Jessica Hannah, Lily Cuzor, Ali Schifani, Claire L. Evans, Jona Bechtolt, Mikey Merrill, Rob Kieswetter, Jenny Lee, Jeffrey Jerusalem, Katy Davidson, Heather Bleemers, Jessica Bianchi, Noah Harmon, Madeleine Baugh, Heidi Darchuk, Michael Chick, Josh Forbes, Anna Magnuson, Amanda Marsalis, Juvenal Rodriguez, John Berry, Neal and Anna Murray, Lesley and Michael Suter, Andrew and Keiko Pogany, Jess Reed, Alie Ward and Georgia Hardstarck, Alexander Wolff, Amanda Kobritz, Brendan Willard, Oystein Greni, Kristen Korven.